EMMA
COOKBO

EMMA'S COOKBOOK

UBS Publishers' Distributors Ltd.

New Delhi • Bombay • Bangalore • Madras •
Calcutta • Patna • Kanpur • London

UBS Publishers' Distributors Ltd.
5 Ansari Road, New Delhi-110 002
Bombay Bangalore Madras Calcutta Patna Kanpur London

First Published **1995**

Cover painting: Jaya Wheaton
Photographs : Sudhir Kasliwal
Illustrations : Alpana Khare, Jaishree Rastogi
Cover design : UBS Art Studio

Designed & Typeset at UBSPD in 11.5 pt New Baskerville
Printed at Nutech Photolithographers, Delhi

Dedicated

To

Rajmata

Gayatri Deviji of Jaipur

Principles of successful cooking

We do not attain perfection by striving to do something out of the common.
Perfection is acquired by doing the common things uncommonly well.

— Mouvry

Acknowledgements

I would like to offer my special gratitude to the Executive Committee: to Rani Vidya Jai Singh, Chairperson of the M.G.D. Girls' School, Jaipur, who first encouraged me to write this cookery book; and to Rani Devika Devi and Thakurani Himmeth Singh for their useful advice and suggestions, and Ms Maya Singh for her valuable help at all times.

I would like to thank Mr Mohd. Ayub Khan for giving his very valuable time to type out all the recipes carefully and patiently.

I would also like to express my gratefulness to the excellent cooks of M.G.D. Girls' School, Jaipur, and to Shri Chet Ram, Shri Panni Ram and Shri Sher Singh, for their kind co-operation and their great efforts in trying out the recipes over and over again till they became perfect. Without their endeavour and perseverance, this book would not have seen the light of day.

The Lilypool
Sawai Ram Singh Road
Jaipur
Rajasthan

Foreword

It is a pleasure to write this foreword to Miss Emma's Cookery Book as I have enjoyed many a meal with her and know the excellence of her cuisine.

An invitation from Miss Lutter was an occasion that one looked forward to eagerly. She was a happy, welcoming and gracious hostess. At her home the company was always congenial and the conversation lively and topical while the meals were delicious.

Miss Emma was in charge of the kitchen and organised these feasts. Whether it was lunch, dinner, tea, snacks or just a glass of fresh fruit juice, everything was beautifully prepared and presented. It was a treat to be a guest in this house and receive such warm hospitality. These are occasions one can never forget.

It is a typically warm hearted gesture on the part of Miss Emma to have written this book of recipes on the occasion of the Golden Jubilee of the Maharani Gayatri Devi School and to have offered the proceeds to the institution.

Thank you Miss Emma.

Gayatri Devi Jaipur.

Rajmata Gayatri Devi of Jaipur

Introduction

This cookery book presents an assorted collection of recipes of dishes from many parts of the world – some garnered from my own travels, some from my friends abroad, and some from our excellent cook, the late Abdul Nazir, who was proficient in international cuisine, and was with us for twenty years.

The recipes have been modified, wherever necessary, so that the dishes can be easily prepared at home, with no fear of not being able to find any of the ingredients in the local market.

I have concentrated basically on dishes which can be made by anyone with a minimum knowledge of the basic culinary techniques and on the kind of food that family and friends normally enjoy.

The proceeds earned from the sale of this book will be given to the M.G.D. Guild.

Emma Hline
M.G.D Girls' School
Jaipur

Contents

Soups 3

Vegetable Stock 3
Bone Stock 4
Clear Soup, Duchesse 4
Egg and Spinach Soup (Chinese) 5
Chicken Broth 5
Venetian Soup (Italy) 6
Chicken Stock with Eggs 6
Cream of Cauliflower Soup 7
Old Fashioned Potato Soup (Holland) 7
Iced Yoghurt Soup (Middle East) 8
Chicken Hotch-Potch (Japanese) 8
Chicken and Yoghurt Soup 9
Ginger Chicken Soup (Chinese) 9
Fish Soup (Chinese) 10
Sweet Corn Soup (Chinese) 10
Grated Potato Soup 11
Burmese Hinjo-Soup 11
Cream of Onion Soup 12
Egg and Cheese Soup (Greek) 12
Soup of Chicken and Mushrooms (Siamese) 13
Cheese Toast (To be served with Cream and Onion Soup) 14
Vegetable Soup 14
Carrot Soup 15
Lemon Soup (Greece) 15

Salads 19

Orange and Apple Salad 19
Cabbage, Spinach and Carrot Salad 20
Green Peas Salad 20
Potato Salad 21
Sardine and Egg Salad 21
Egg, Beetroot and Radish Salad 22
Egg and Spinach Mould Salad 22
Cheese Salad 23
Cucumber Salad (Russian) 23
Orange and Cucumber Salad 24
Grape and Pineapple Salad 24
Apple and Banana Salad 25
Stuffed Tomato Salad 25
Chicken Salad 26
Fish Salad 26
Chicken and Walnut Salad 27
Cabbage, Apple and Orange Salad 28
Cole Slaw 28
Salad Loaf 29
Chilled Fruit Salad 29
Honey Fruit Salad 30
Japanese Salad 31
Cucumber Salad (Thai) 31

Fowl, Fish and Meat 35

Steamed Minced Pork (Burmese) 35
Meat Curry (Burmese) 36
Fish Lethoke (Burmese Fish Salad) 36
Almond-Chicken 37
Burmese Meat Balachaung 38
Burmese Chicken Curry 39
Chicken with Rice Cooked in Chicken Broth (Thai) 40
Chinese Chicken Chop Suey 41
Fried Fish in Cheese 41
Hsan Byoke (Burmese Fish Soup with Rice) 42
Tomato Curry (Burmese) 43
Fried Roselle (Burmese) 43
Stuffed Brinjal (Burmese) 44
Fried Fish with Ginger Sauce (Siamese) 45
Devilled Grilled Fish 45
Hon of Prawns (Siamese) 46
Shrimp Toast (Thai) 46
Paprika Chicken 47
Grilled Pork Chops with Orange Slices 47
Chicken in Sour-Cream Gravy (Norway) 48
Garnish for Fish Preparations 48
Burmese Chicken Kauksewe 49
Burmese Prawn Balachaung 50
Fish Mousse 50
Fish Kababs 51
Creamy Lemon Chicken (Italy) 51
West African Groundnut Stew 52
Bahmi (A Chinese dish popular in Indonesia) 53
Fried Spring Chicken 54
Creamed Chicken 54
Spaghetti Bolognese 55

Mutton Chops 55
Fish Baked in Banana Leaves (Indonesian) 56
Chinese Fried Fish Chinois 56
Pineapple with Meat or with Veal (A Danish way) 57
Cubes of Mutton in Batter (Malayan) 58
Fish Fritters 59
Poulet a la Creole (The French West Indies) 59
A Jam Panggang 60
Hawaiian Chops 60
Lamb Chops (Fried) with Cheese and Macaroni 61
Scrambled Fish 62

Eggs **65**

Baked Eggs with Cream and Toast 68
Hurry-up Curried Eggs 68
Surprise Eggs 69
Fluffy Egg 69
Swiss Eggs 70
Sweet Potato Croquettes 70
Fried Egg Fingers 71
Cheese Scrambled Eggs 71
French Toast 72
Eggs in Nests 72
Cheese Toast (French) 73
Cheese Straws 73
Burmese Egg Dish 74
Milk Toast (USA) 75

Rice **79**

Coconut Rice (Burmese) 79
Cheese Rice 80
Savoury Steamed Rice (Chinese) 80
Anchovy Rice 81
Golden Rice 81
Fried Rice (Chinese) I 82
Fried Rice (Chiense) II 82
Kedgere 83
Malayan Fried Balls of Rice 83
Rice Milan Style 84
Nasigoreng – Fried Rice (Indonesian) 85
Buttered Rice 85
Almond Rice 86
Rice Border 86

Vegetarian Recipes **89**

Stuffed Onions 89
Creamy Jacket Potatoes 90
Potato with Baked Eggs 91
Cream Potatoes 91
Burmese Pickle (Thanai) 92
Sweet Corn Toast 93
Brinjal Bartha 93
Spinach Rolls 94
Aubergine Caviar (Russian) 95
Cream Cheese 95
Green Capsicum Rounds 96
Potato Pancakes 96
Belgian Cucumber 97
Serbian Cabbage (Belgrade) 97
Roast Pumpkin 98
Onion Bhaji 98
Corn Fritters 99
Banana Mayonnaise 99
Sweet and Sour Paneer with Sprouted Dal 100
French Fried Potatoes 101
Fried Loki (Burmese) 101
Riced Potatoes 102
Harvard Beets 102
Mushroom Curry (Burmese) 103
Creamed Peas 103
Cheese Moulds 104
Spinach with Cheese 105
Spicy Cheese Dip 105
Dietetic Fruit Dish (Muesli) Apple Muesli 106
Cooked Radishes with Cheese 106

Sandwiches **109**

Cheese and Banana Sandwiches 109
Golden Ham Sandwiches 110
Egg Sandwiches 110
Sandwiches with Chicken Left-overs 111
Date and Nut Sandwiches 111
Coconut-Cashewnut Sandwiches 112
Peanut Butter and Pickle Sandwiches 112
Cucumber Sandwiches 113
Chicken and Egg Sandwiches 113
Tuna Sandwiches Deluxe 114
Cream Cheese-Raisin Sandwiches 114
Cheese and Orange Marmalade Sandwiches 115
Sardine-Cream Cheese Sandwiches 115
Salad Loaf 116
Curried Chicken-Ham Sandwiches 116
Fried Hot Sandwiches 117
Almond-Chicken Sandwiches 117
Sardine-Cream Cheese Sandwiches 118
Sweet Corn Sandwich 118

Dips 121
Curry Dip (Bahamas) 121
Cheese Balls 122
Summer Special 122
Ham and Marmalade Spread 123
Pineapple Dip 123
Salami Kababs 124
Watermelon Cocktail 124
Celery and Ham 125
Bacon, Peanut Butter Dip 125
Sardine Strips 125
Dates and Nut Spread 126
Speedy Tuna Dunk 126
Cheddar Dip 127
Overstuffed Eggs 127
Shrimp Butter 128
Chilli Toast 128
Shrimp on Toast (Chinese) 129
Curry Relish 129
Cheese Popcorn 129
Mango Fool 130
Simple Fruit Cocktail 130
Plum Juice 130

Sweets and Puddings 133
Peach Melba 133
The Story of Peach Melba 134
Floating Island 134
Brandy Rings 135
Banana Bread 135
Banana Fritters 136
Pineapple Fromage (Sweden) 136
Condensed Milk Toffee 137
Date and Walnut Fudge (Middle East) 137
Icecream Cakewiches 138
Treacle Syrup 138
Date Pudding 139
Fruit Pudding (Sweden) 139
Sultana Pudding 140
Banana Cream (As served in Belgium) 140
Caramel Square (Chinese) 141
Garlic Bread 142
Coffee Jelly 142
Coconut Custard (Malayan) 143
Mocha Coffee (Austria) 143
Pumpkin and Walnuts (Middle East) 144
Brandy or Ginger Snaps 144
Peanut Cookies 145
Burmese Coconut Blanc-Mange 145
Brown Bread 146
Pineapple Balls 146
Peach Baskets 147
Sago Sweet (Burmese) 148

Sauces, Dressings and Miscellaneous 151
Mayonnaise Salad Dressing 151
Homemade Mustard 152
French Dressing 152
Pickled Pineapple (To serve with polutry) 153
Tartar Sauce – I 153
Tartar Sauce – II
Alispice 154
Chocolate Sauce 155
Butter Sauce 155
Celery Sauce 156
White Sauce 156
Mushroom Sauce 157
Christmas Pudding Sauce 157
Apple Sauce 158
White Wine Sauce 158
Mint Sauce 159
Ginger Sauce (Siamese) 160
Ginger Pickle (Thai) 160
Cheese Sauce 161
Dream Puris 161

A Note of Wine 162

SOUPS

Soups are the most economical, most substantial and the easiest of foods to prepare.

Vegetable Stock

Foundation	:	625 gms vegetables such as carrots, turnips, celery, etc., except cabbage. 4 cups cold water.
Flavouring vegetables	:	1 small onion
Seasoning	:	1 level teaspoon salt, 4 white peppercorns.

1. Boil the water with the peppercorns and salt.
2. Clean the vegetables, cut them into thin slices, and put them into the boiling liquid.
3. Cook at simmering point for 30-40 minutes, until the vegetables are soft but not broken.
4. Strain, allow to cool, and use for vegetable soups, vegetarian cooking or for general cookery purposes.

Bone Stock

Foundation	:	625 gms cooked or uncooked bones of meat, poultry or fish. 4 cups cold water.
Flavouring vegetables	:	1 small onion, 1 small carrot.
Seasoning	:	1 level teaspoon salt, 5 white peppercorns.

1. Wash the bones and chop into small pieces. Put in pan with well-fitting lid. Cover with water and add seasoning.
2. Bring slowly to the boil and add whole vegetables.
3. Simmer for 2-3 hours or until the bones are dry and pitted with small holes.
4. Strain through a coarse strainer into a clean basin, cover and allow to cool.
5. Remove the fat from the surface and keep the stock in the refrigerator until required.

Clear Soup, Duchesse

4 cups chicken stock

1 tablespoon parsley or celery

¼ cup diced chicken

1 tablespoon sago

1. Boil stock and add sago. Simmer for 20 minutes. Add stock, chicken and parsley and season to taste.
2. A little sherry may be stirred in before serving.

   Serves 4.

Egg and Spinach Soup (Chinese)

250 gm spinach leaves, washed, drained and chopped

6 cups stock

Pinch of white pepper

2 eggs, lightly beaten

1. Bring soup stock to a boil, season with white pepper. Add spinach leaves and pour beaten egg slowly into soup. Do not overcook.
2. Remove from heat and serve immediately.

   Serves 7 to 8.

Chicken Broth

4 cups chicken stock

1½ tablespoons rice

2 onion leeks (chopped finely)

2 tablespoons parsley (chopped)

1. Wash and chop leeks and parsley.
2. Add leeks and rice to chicken stock, and simmer for 45 minutes.
3. Pour soup over parsley in soup bowl and serve.

   Serves 4 to 5.

Venetian Soup (Italy)

6 cups or 3 pints of cold chicken stock
6 slices of hot toasted bread
3 eggs
4 tablespoons cream or 3 tablespoons flour

1. Beat the egg-yolks with the cream/flour. Stir this into the stock. Bring almost to boiling point slowly, then remove immediately from the fire.
2. Place the toasted bread (1 slice each) in 6 soup bowls, cover with the hot soup and serve.
Serves 6.

Chicken Stock with Eggs

This is one of the regular station soups, very simple to make, nourishing and very good to eat.

1 egg
1 slice of fried bread
Grated cheese
Salt and pepper
Boiling chicken stock

1. Place a slice of hot fried bread in the soup plate. Sprinkle this generously with grated cheese, add one raw egg and plenty of salt and pepper. Pour the boiling chicken stock. (It must be hot enough to poach the egg.)
2. Some people prefer to poach the egg before putting it into the soup plate so that the egg is sufficiently cooked.
Serves 1.

Cream of Cauliflower Soup

2 medium-sized cauliflowers

1½ tablespoons flour

1 cup of hot milk

8 cups stock

2 egg yolks

Salt and pepper to taste

1. Heat stock and add sprigs of washed cauliflower and flour mixed with a little water. Boil till tender and sieve.
2. Dilute egg yolks with milk and add to stock.
3. Season with salt and pepper and heat well till soup thickens. Garnish with parsley.

   Serves 6 to 8.

Old Fashioned Potato Soup (Holland)

8 potatoes (cubed)
4 cups milk
1 tablespoon butter
Salt and pepper
1 egg (well beaten)
½ cup flour
¼ cup milk

1. Boil and mash the potatoes until soft. Drain all the water. Add the milk and heat thoroughly. Season to taste.
2. Work the butter into the flour. Then add the egg and milk, using only enough milk to make the mixture thin enough to drop into the hot milk. Drop by teaspoonfuls into hot milk.
3. Cover the saucepan and cook for about 10 minutes. Serve at once.

   Serves 6 to 8.

Iced Yoghurt Soup (Middle East)

4 cups yoghurt
A little finely chopped mint
Seedless raisins (a handful)
1 cup chopped and peeled cucumber
1 cup cold water
Salt and pepper to taste

1. Beat the yoghurt until smooth. Add salt, pepper, mint, a handful of seedless raisins, cucumber and water.
2. When all these ingredients are well blended put the soup in the refrigerator and leave until it is chilled.
   Serves 4 to 6.

Chicken Hotch-Potch (Japanese)

1 cup chicken meat from the legs cut into small pieces
3 cups chicken stock
3 Chinese mushrooms (soaked in water)
3 eggs
1 teaspoon sugar
1 teaspoon soya sauce
1 teaspoon salt
1 tablespoon green peas (fresh)
10 spinach leaves (washed and chopped)
A few drops of lemon juice

1. Heat the stock with sugar and soya sauce and add the well stirred eggs to the liquid. Stir and put aside.
2. Place the chicken pieces, the mushrooms (sliced) peas and spinach in a bowl and cover. Steam until meat is done. Add the chicken mixture to the soup and heat. Add a few drops of lemon juice and serve.
   Serves 4 to 6.

Chicken and Yoghurt Soup

8 cups chicken stock
1 tablespoon flour
2 tablespoons rice
1 cup yoghurt
2 beaten egg-yolks
2 tablespoons butter
1 tablespoon chopped mint
2 cups water
Salt and pepper

1. Bring the stock to a boil, add rice and cook it for 15 minutes. Season with salt and pepper.
2. In another pan mix the flour, yoghurt, egg-yolks and one pint of water. Cook slowly until almost boiling. Add rice and stock. Stir and simmer for a further 5 minutes.
3. Melt the butter, add the mint and pour this dressing over the soup when it is in the plates.
   Serves 10 to 12.

Ginger Chicken Soup (Chinese)

1 broiler chicken cut into small pieces
4 inches fresh ginger
6 cups water
Pinch of salt
Pinch of Aji-no-moto

1. Wash, clean and put chicken pieces with fresh ginger (cut into small slivers) into cold water to cook at low heat until the meat is tender and the soup is cooked. Add salt and Aji-no-moto to taste.
2. Serve with rice.
   Serves 6.

Fish Soup (Chinese)

2 cups shredded fish (Pomfret is the best)

1 egg

1 tablespoon flour

1 teaspoon vinegar

1 teaspoon soya sauce

4 cups hot water

Salt if needed – a dash of Aji-no-moto

1. Add 4 cups of water to fish and let it boil.
2. Add flour for thickening and soya sauce.
3. Beat eggs and stir into boiling soup. Add vinegar and serve.
4. Garnish with chopped onion leeks.

Serves 4 to 6.

Sweet Corn Soup (Chinese)

250 gm chicken breast
1 small tin sweet corn
1 inch fresh ginger
1 egg
A dash of Aji-no-moto
1 teaspoon wine or sherry (optional)
Salt to taste

Shred the chicken and season with salt and Aji-no-moto. Cut the ginger into small strips and fry in a saucepan in a little oil. Add the shredded chicken and fry for a few minutes. Bring the chicken stock to a boil and add to the fried meat and ginger. Add the wine, cover the pan and simmer until the chicken is tender. Add sweet corn and simmer for five minutes longer. Remove from fire, add the beaten egg, stir well and serve.
Serves 4.

Grated Potato Soup

6 cups soup stock
4 thin slices garlic
2 onion leeks sliced
1 medium onion, minced
6 uncooked potatoes, grated
Salt and pepper

1. Heat stock to a boil and add the rest of the ingredients.
2. Simmer for 20 minutes or until vegetables are tender.
3. Add salt and pepper.
   Serves 8

Burmese Hinjo – Soup

Sorrel leaves (two handfuls)
2 medium sized onions
3 cloves garlic
6 cups water
Salt to taste
½ cup dried or fresh prawns

1. Wash prawns and grind. Peel and slice very fine the garlic and onions.
2. Put these in a saucepan with 6 cups of water and boil for 5-8 minutes. Add the leaves and cook till tender. Add salt to taste.
3. Finely shredded cabbage or drumstick leaves or loki (*white gourd*) sliced thin, can be used for this Burmese soup.
   Serves 4

Cream of Onion Soup

1 cup onions
1 tablespoon butter
2 tablespoons flour
2½ cups milk
1 egg yolk (optional)
1 tablespoon cream
Salt, pepper and a dash of Aji-no-moto

1. Chop and gently fry the onions in the hot butter until tender, but do not brown.
2. Add the flour and mix it well, then cook for a minute.
3. Add milk and cook gently for about 20 minutes.
4. Mix egg yolks and cream together, add a little soup, then return all to the saucepan and heat without boiling.
5. Season to taste.
   Serve with cheese toast. (*Recipe on page 14*)
   Serves 4

Egg and Cheese Soup (Greek)

4 cups chicken stock

4 egg yolks

1 cup grated cheese

1. Heat the stock.
2. Beat the eggs, add the cheese and stir over a very low heat in the soup pan until the cheese has melted.
3. Slowly pour in the hot chicken stock, stirring all the time, heat again and serve.

Soup of Chicken and Mushrooms (Siamese)

1 small chicken (broiler)

2 cups fresh mushrooms or tinned mushrooms

Coriander roots (2 or 3)

Peppercorns (6)

4 cloves of garlic

Cooking fat

Chicken stock (8 cups)

Fish sauce (Nam-pla) available in Calcutta and Delhi

1. Clean and chop coarsely 2 cups of fresh mushrooms. Soak in cold water.
2. Cook chicken in chicken stock till tender, then remove flesh, and cut it into small pieces. Keep between two plates. Cut and chop the bones. Return to the pot. Let it simmer for about one hour. If fresh mushrooms are used, they should be parboiled.
3. Pound together the garlic, pepper and coriander roots. Add chicken pieces and *nam-pla,* stirring well.
4. Add stock and bring to boiling point. Then add the mushrooms.
5. Cover and allow to boil for a few minutes. Serve very hot in individual cups.

   Serves 8 to 10

CHEESE TOAST (To be served with Cream of Onion Soup)

1. Butter 5 or 6 slices of thin crustless white bread.
2. Mix 1 cup grated cheese with egg white and spread this mixture generously on the bread and bake at 435ºF for 5-10 minutes until crisp and golden. Cut into squares and serve hot.

VEGETABLE SOUP

1 cup mixed vegetables in season (eg. peas, carrots, beans, spring onions)

2 tablespoons butter

2 cups milk

1 level tablespoon flour

Salt and a dash of Aji-no-moto

Cooking time – 25 minutes.

1. Heat the butter in the pan.
2. Toss in the vegetables and then add water.
3. Cook until tender.
4. Blend the flour with the milk, add to vegetables.
5. Reheat until smooth, season.
6. Serve with fresh cream if you like.

Serves 4

Carrot Soup

1 large onion

2 skinned tomatoes

1½ oz butter

4 cups white stock or water

½ kg carrots, peeled and chopped

1 clove garlic, crushed

Salt and pepper – a dash of Aji-no-moto

1½ tablespoons of flour

1 cup milk

Parsley or mint

1. Chop the onion and tomatoes and toss in the butter.
2. Add the stock or water and the carrots and garlic.
3. Season well and simmer for 30-40 minutes until the carrots are tender.
4. Blend the flour and milk and work until smooth. Bring to the boil, stirring constantly, and cook until thickened.
5. Sieve the carrot mixture, blend with the thickened milk; reheat and top with chopped parsley.
6. Serve with fried bread croutons.

   Serves 4-5.

Lemon Soup (Greece)

1. This typically Greek soup consists of good chicken stock with a little rice and is simmered for 10 minutes till the rice is cooked.
2. Before serving, the yolks of 2 eggs, diluted with a little of the warm stock, are mixed in, and the juice of 1½ limes.
3. Stir for a few minutes and serve with croutons of fried bread.

SALADS

The term salad comes from the French salade and is a derivation of salt-sel. Salads are recommended all the year round for health and slimming.

Orange and Apple Salad

1 small cabbage
1 apple
1 stick celery
1 beetroot
8 walnuts (chopped)
1 cup mayonnaise
1 orange

1. Remove the large leaves of the cabbage; shred the heart, wash it well and drain; mix with it some finely chopped apple, celery, orange and beetroot.
2. Serve in a salad bowl, cover with mayonnaise and sprinkle the surface with chopped walnuts.

Cabbage, Spinach and Carrot Salad

1 cabbage
Young carrots
Spinach (same quantity as cabbage)
1 onion (grated)
1 hard-boiled egg
1 cup mayonnaise

1. Strip off the dark outer leaves of the cabbage, wash it well, drain and chop the heart as finely as possible.
2. Wash the carrots and grate a quantity equal to the weight of the shredded cabbage. Wash the spinach well, drain it and chop very fine. Add the grated onion.
3. Mix all the above ingredients thoroughly, place them in a salad bowl, pour mayonnaise over just before serving and garnish with slices of hard-boiled egg.

Green Peas Salad

3 cups cooked green peas
1 cup mayonnaise
Lettuce
2 hard-boiled eggs

Mix the peas with mayonnaise and pile in the centre of a dish, surround with shredded lettuce, and scatter over the surface of the peas some powdered yolk of hard-boiled eggs. Chop the whites and sprinkle them on the lettuce.

A 1944 report stated that peas taken from the 3300-year-old tomb of Tutankhamen had been sown in Florida, and they germinated!

Potato Salad

8 medium-sized boiled potatoes, cooled and sliced
1 cup mayonnaise
½ cup spring onions
Parsley or celery
2 hard-boiled eggs

Chop the onions very fine and mix them with the sliced potatoes. Stir some mayonnaise into them and heap onto little dishes. Chop the eggs and scatter them, with some chopped parsley over the potatoes.

Potato (Apple of the Earth): The actual word potato is a derivation of "promme de terre". Potatoes contain a large surplus quantity of base which render very valuable service in the fight against uric acid, especially when the potatoes are cooked properly. The best way is to cook them in their skins.

Sardine and Egg Salad

1 tin sardines
Lettuce
2 hard-boiled eggs
3 teaspoons French dressing

1. Remove the bones from the sardines. Wash, drain and shred the lettuce.
2. Place the lettuce in a salad bowl, arrange the sardines on it, surrounded with a border of sliced, hard-boiled eggs and cover with French dressing.

Egg, Beetroot and Radish Salad

2 cooked beetroots

2 radishes

1 medium cucumber

2 hard-boiled eggs

1 onion

Lettuce

1 cup mayonnaise

1. Peel and slice one or two beetroots and cut the slices into match-like strips, mix with some thinly sliced cucumber, radish, chopped hard-boiled egg and chopped onion.
2. Blend these with mayonnaise and pile on a bed of shredded lettuce.

Egg and Spinach Mould Salad

1 kg spinach

Pepper and salt

2 hard-boiled eggs

1 cup mayonnaise

Cook spinach until tender, drain well and press into either one large or several small moulds, and when quite cold and set turn out, decorate with slices of hard-boiled egg and pour thick mayonnaise over the salad.

Cheese Salad

A lettuce

8 medium-sized cooked potatoes

Salt and pepper

1 tablespoonful mustard

1 cup grated cheese

Olive oil or salad oil

A little vinegar

1. Wash the lettuce well and allow it to drain thoroughly, slice the potatoes thin.
2. Mix the mustard, salt and pepper and grated cheese. Add the oil gradually until a stiff paste is formed, then add slowly a little vinegar. Shred the lettuce and lay it on a dish surrounded with sliced potatoes and pour the cheese mixture over. *Serves 4-6.*

Cucumber Salad (Russian)

1 large cucumber

1 clove garlic

Vinegar (1 teaspoonful to 1 tablespoon)

½ cup cream

Paprika (red chilli powder)

Salt and pepper to taste

Sugar to taste

1. Slice the cucumber thinly, sprinkle with salt and leave in a dish for 1 hour. Put vinegar in a salad bowl, add a crushed clove of garlic, mix and press down in the vinegar. Add sugar, then add pepper. Mix thoroughly.
2. Drain the cucumber well – add it to the dressing, taste for flavour. If desired add more vinegar and sugar. Now add the cream, sprinkle the top with paprika. Serve very cold.

   Serves 4-6.

Orange and Cucumber Salad

3 large oranges
1 large cucumber
3 or 4 good small tomatoes
Watercress

1. Cut away the skins of the oranges so that the fibre and seeds are removed.
2. Slice the cucumber thinly, halve the tomatoes.
3. Arrange on a dish.
4. Garnish with the prepared watercress.

This can be served with French dressing and is an excellent salad for use with pork, ham or cheese.

Serves 4.

Grape and Pineapple Salad

1 tin pineapple slices
A lettuce
2 cups grapes
24 glacé cherries
1 cup cream

Wash and dry the lettuce, arrange the leaves of the heart on a flat dish or shallow bowl, lay the pineapple slices on the leaves, surround each with grapes, which have been cut in halves and the seeds removed. Put a spoonful of whipped cream in the centre of each slice of pineapple and place three or four glacé cherries on each.

Serves 10-12.

Apple and Banana Salad

1 bunch lettuce
2 apples
2 bananas
Juice of one lemon
¼ cup cream
2 teaspoons walnuts

1. Peel, core and cut the apples into dice and mix with thinly sliced bananas. Pour lemon juice over and stir together.
2. Lay the fruit on young lettuce leaves, pour whipped cream over and cover the surface with a sprinkling of chopped nuts.

Stuffed Tomato Salad

4 large firm tomatoes
2 apples
1 cup mayonnaise (thick)
½ cup chopped nuts
¼ cup celery, chopped

Cut the tomatoes across into halves and scoop the seeds out of each half. Chop finely and mix with some apples, celery and nuts. Stuff each half of the tomato with the mixture, and stand them on a bed of lettuce and pour thick mayonnaise over each.

In olden and possibly more romantic days, the French called tomatoes 'pomme d' amour', and these "apples of love" were the fashionable thing for a suitor to give his lady fair. Sometimes in a solid gold replica!

Chicken Salad

Remains of cold chicken

Apples, celery, nuts

Mayonnaise and whipped cream

Chop some cold chicken, removing all skin, bone and gristle, dice some apples and celery and mix with the chicken. Arrange on a dish. Add a covering of finely chopped nuts and pour over some mayonnaise mixed with whipped cream.

Fish Salad

2 cups cold boiled fish (surmai or pomfret)

1 cup celery, cucumber

2 hard-boiled eggs

Pepper and salt

½ cup mayonnaise

Flake the fish, removing all skin and bone. Mix with an equal quantity of diced celery and cucumber.

Season with pepper and salt and arrange on a dish.

Cover with a layer of chopped hard-boiled eggs, and pour some mayonnaise over.

Serves 4.

Chicken and Walnut Salad

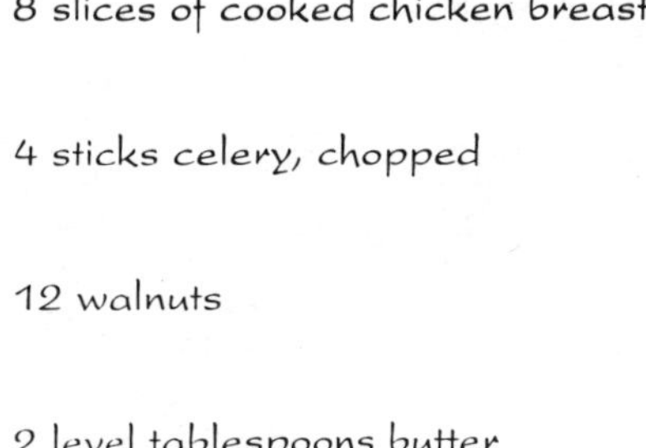

8 slices of cooked chicken breast

4 sticks celery, chopped

12 walnuts

2 level tablespoons butter

Lettuce leaves

½ cup mayonnaise

Brown the walnuts in the butter, chop them and mix with the chicken and celery. Arrange on lettuce leaves, cover with mayonnaise. Serve chilled.

Serves 6 to 8 .

Cabbage, Apple and Orange Salad

12 oz shredded cabbage

2 oranges

1 apple

2 tablespoons lime juice

1 cucumber and tomato to garnish

1 cup mayonnaise

Peel the oranges and cut finely across the fruit to make very small sections. Grate the apple. Mix cabbage, apple and oranges with lime juice. Arrange in a salad bowl, garnish with cucumber and tomato and serve with mayonnaise.

Cole Slaw

About 500 gm white cabbage

½ cup French dressing (more can be added if need be)

Cut off the outside leaves of the cabbage, cut out the main stem and the thickest stems in the leaves.

Shred and soak in cold water for 1 hour. Drain it and mix with French dressing. This can be varied by the addition of raw chopped apple and sultanas.

Salad Loaf

1 loaf bread (1 lb)
1 cup cooked chicken (chopped)
1 cup cooked ham (chopped)
2 cups mayonnaise
Salt and pepper
Cream cheese

1. To make, trim crusts from loaf of day-old bread, slice off top and scoop out inside, leaving a ¾ inch shell all around.
2. Fill with chicken, ham mixed with mayonnaise, replace and tie on top slice and chill.
3. Frost with seasoned cream cheese and chill again.
4. Serve on a platter and slice like a loaf of bread.

Chilled Fruit Salad

1 egg yolk
50 gm sugar
Juice of 1 lemon
Salt
3 slices tinned pineapple, diced
½ small tin cherries (½ cup)
150 gm grapes, peeled and seeded
50 gm almonds, blanched and chopped, and cream ½ cup

Mix the sugar, cream and egg yolk with pinch of salt.
Cook until thick. Mix with the other ingredients.
Leave in a refrigerator for 24 hours. Serve on lettuce with mayonnaise or as a sweet with whipped cream.
Serves 3 to 4.

Honey Fruit Salad

4 large oranges

2 cups seedless green grapes

2 cups seedless red grapes (use black grapes instead)

1/2 cup halved pitted dates

1/2 cup orange juice (fresh)

2 tablespoons honey or more if needed

Whipped cream to garnish

1. With small paring knife, peel oranges removing the white membranes. Cut oranges in thin slices, then halve.

2 Place in a large bowl with grapes and dates – set aside.

3. In small glass bowl, combine orange juice and honey, pour over fruits mix lightly to coat, cover and chill.

4. Garnish with whipped cream.

Serves 8.

Japanese Salad

2 or 3 small lettuce leaves for each plate

6 slices of pineapple (fresh or tinned)

3 tomatoes

3 oranges

3 pears

Whipped cream

1. Place some lettuce leaves on a plate, then a slice of pineapple.
2. Top with small pieces of tomato, orange, pear (and other fresh fruits as available).
3. Garnish with whipped cream.

Cucumber Salad (Thai)

2 Cucumber (peeled and thickly sliced)

1/4 cup red onion sliced thin

1 cup vinegar

2 tablespoons sugar

1 red chilli sliced

1 teaspoon salt

1. Put vinegar, sugar, salt in pot, heat over low heat, let cool.
2. When the vinegar is cool, add cucumber and red chilli sliced, red onion and mix well.

   Serve.

FOWL, FISH AND MEAT

Steamed Minced Pork (Burmese)

500 gm pork loin, lean with fat

4 eggs

6 pods garlic

4 onions

Salt to taste

15 fresh prawns sprinkled with ½ teaspoon lime juice

1. Wash and mince the pork.
2. Finely slice garlic and onions.
3. Beat eggs and mix with pork, finely sliced garlic and onions.
4. Add prawns and salt to taste.
5. Put in steamer over boiling water and steam till well cooked. Serve with plain rice and any vegetable curry or fried roselle.

   Serves 4-6.

Meat Curry (Burmese)

½ kg meat or pork

4 tablespoons cooking oil

½ tablespoon salt

⅛ teaspoon turmeric (haldi) powder

¼ teaspoon chilli powder

2 onions

2 cloves garlic

Small piece fresh ginger

1½ tablespoons Chinese soya sauce

1. Cut meat in 1 inch strips.
2. Grind onions, garlic and ginger into a paste.
3. Put oil in saucepan. When hot put in ground paste and other seasonings (salt, *haldi*, chilli powder and Chinese soya sauce).
4. Add meat and cook till brown.
5. Add water to cover and simmer for 30 minutes or until the meat is tender. Serve with rice.

   Serves 4.

Fish Lethoke (Burmese Fish Salad)

Fish (any good fish available in India)

3 tablespoons oil

2 onions

1 dessert spoon gram flour (besan), roasted

1 tablespoon fish sauce

1 lime

3 tender lemon grass leaves (or green coriander leaves)

1. Scoop out the flesh of fish and grind till smooth.
2. Make small balls of this, a teaspoonful to each ball.
3. Place in boiling water over fire. These will float when cooked. Slice thinly.
4. Fry the thinly sliced onions in oil.
5. Mix together thoroughly the fish sauce, gram flour and lime juice and pour over the fish.
6. Garnish with fried onions and cut leaves of lemon grass (if not available, use green coriander leaves).

   Serves 4 to 6.

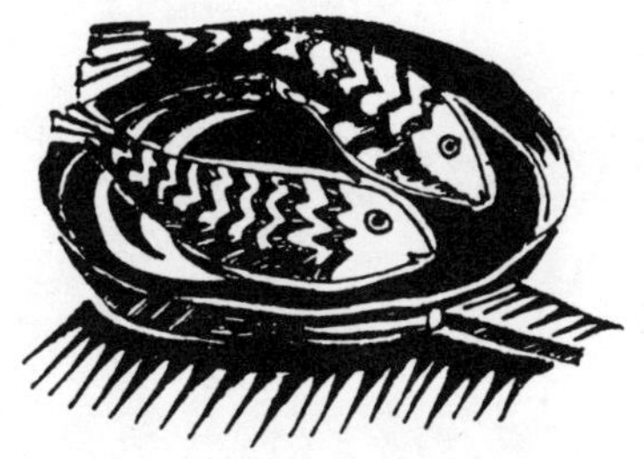

Almond-Chicken

2 tablespoons butter

$^1/_3$ cup ground salted almonds

1 cup finely chopped cooked chicken

2 tablespoons seedless green grapes (cut fine)

1 tablespoon mayonnaise

A dash of salt

Combine and blend the above ingredients with the mayonnaise and adding salt according to your taste.

BURMESE MEAT BALACHAUNG

1½ kg good mutton
100 gm fresh ginger for juice
1 inch of fresh ginger
1 teaspoon Aji-no-moto
2 teaspoons fish sauce
A pinch of turmeric
12 red chillies
4 pods garlic
4 big onions (sliced)
2 cups oil (refined oil)
Salt to taste
2 cups of water

1. Wash the meat and cut into large pieces.
2. Marinate the meat with ginger juice, Ali-no-moto, turmeric and fish sauce for ½ hour.
3. Boil the meat in 2 cups of water until all the water has been absorbed.
4. When cool, pound and shred the meat.
5. Heat oil and fry the sliced onions until crisp and set aside.
6. Grind together the chillies, garlic and ginger and cook in the same oil for 5 minutes.
7. Add the shredded meat and cook until the meat is crisp.
8. When cool add the fried onions.
9. It is delicious with rice or puris.

Burmese Chicken Curry

2 chickens of $1\frac{1}{4}$ kg each

½ cup oil

3 red chillies

3 cloves garlic

3 onions

1 teaspoon salt

1 teaspoon curry powder

1 tablespoon Chinese soya sauce

5 cups of water

Pinch of turmeric (haldi) powder

3 bay leaves

1 stick cinnamon

1. Have chickens cleaned and drawn. Cut into suitable sizes.
2. Mix turmeric powder, curry powder, and Chinese soya sauce, and rub into the chicken.
3. Grind together chillies, garlic and onions to a paste. Fry in cooked oil till brown.
4. Add spiced meat and cook till it sizzles. Add 5 cups of water.
5. Throw in 3 bay leaves and a stick of cinnamon. Simmer till tender, and the water is reduced to half. Serve with coconut rice.

   Serves 8

Chicken with Rice Cooked in Chicken Broth (Thai)

2 chicken breasts or thighs

3 cups water

2 tablespoons crushed coriander roots

1½ cups rice

3 tablespoons cooking oil

10 slightly crushed garlic cloves

5 peeled cucumbers

1 teaspoon salt

1 tablespoon coriander leaves for garnishing

1. Boil 3 cups water with the salt and coriander. Add chicken to the boiling water and cook until the chicken is done – skim off froth, and use low heat to get a clear broth.
2. Remove chicken from pot, bone it and cut it into thin slices. Strain broth and save for cooking rice.
3. Wash rice, drain off water and keep it aside.
4. Heat oil in a frying pan. Add garlic and rice and fry for 3 minutes over medium heat, then transfer rice into a pot with 2 ½ cups chicken broth and cook until rice is done.
5. Spoon rice into soup bowls, top with sliced chicken and garnish with coriander leaves. Serve with sliced cucumber.

Serves 4.

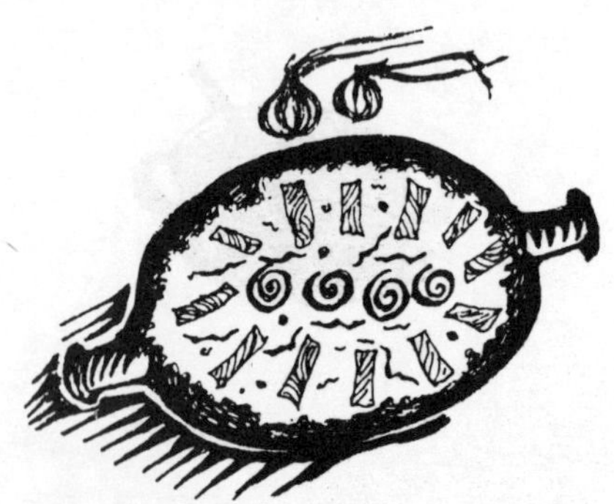

Chinese Chicken Chop Suey

2 oz mushrooms
½ pint stock
2 chicken legs
6 oz sliced onions
12 oz bean shoots or fresh beans
4 oz thinly sliced bamboo shoots (optional)
A pinch of sugar
1 level teaspoon cornflour
Fat or oil to fry
Seasoning: A few drops soya sauce to garnish fried omelette.

1. Chop mushrooms finely and soak in stock.
2. Cut chicken from bones in neat pieces, use about 8 oz.
3. Fry chicken pieces, onions, beans and bamboo shoots for a few minutes.
4. Add the mushrooms and stock together with seasoning, soya sauce, sugar and cook gently for about 30 minutes.
5. Blend cornflour with very little stock, add to ingredients in pan, bring to the boil and cook for 1 minute.
6. Pile on to hot dish and serve with fried noodles or fried noodles or fried rice. Garnish with strips of fried omelette.

Fried Fish in Cheese

1. An excellent way to vary fish and to add extra food value if the fish are small in size is to coat them with egg and a mixture of bread crumbs and grated cheese.
2. Fry in shallow fat until crisp and golden brown.

HSAN BYOKE (Burmese Fish Soup with Rice)

1 kg fish (any good fish available in India)

8 cups water

¼ cup rice

1 cup shredded cabbage

2 tablespoons chopped celery

¼ teaspoon Aji-no-moto

Salt, pepper, soya sauce to taste

1. Wash and clean the fish. Boil bones and skin in water for ½ hour. Strain and throw away bones.
2. Wash rice thoroughly and boil in fish stock for ¼ hour or more.
3. Cut the fish into bite-sized pieces and mix with salt, pepper and soya sauce. Add fish to rice stock and cook for another ¼ hour.
4. Add vegetables and boil for another 5 minutes. Be careful not to overcook vegetables.
5. Serve hot in bowls.

Instead of fish, you may use an equal amount of chicken, pork ribs or duck. Use any vegetables in season, thus adding colour to the dish.

Serves 8 to 10.

TOMATO CURRY (Burmese)

15 to 20 good tomatoes
1 cup dried prawns, pounded (or fresh prawns, chopped)
4 onions, sliced
1 pod garlic, sliced
½ teaspoon turmeric (haldi) powder
½ teaspoon salt
3 tablespoons oil, use sesame, (til) oil
4 tablespoons water

1. Cut each tomato in quarters.
2. Add pounded prawns, sliced onions, garlic, *haldi* and salt with the tomatoes.
3. Pour oil and water over the ingredients in the saucepan.
4. Cook till the water is absorbed. Serve with plain rice and fried loki (white gourd).
   Serves 4.

FRIED ROSELLE (Burmese)

½ kg roselle leaves
4 tablespoons cooking oil
½ cup dried prawn powder
½ teaspoon turmeric (haldi) powder
1 onion, sliced
6 cloves garlic, sliced
5 green chillies
½ teaspoon fish paste (available in Delhi and Calcutta) or fish sauce
1 teaspoon salt

Wash roselle leaves. Heat cooking oil in pan. Put roselle leaves with all the ingredients into pan, stirring constantly till cooked and dry. Serve with rice and curry.
Serves 4.

Stuffed Brinjal (Burmese)

4 good sized brinjals (eggplant)
1 cup dried prawns
1½ cups oil
3 medium sized onions
2 pods garlic
3 dried chillies
½ inch fresh ginger
A little turmeric (haldi) powder
Salt to taste
½ teaspoon fish paste or fish sauce (available in Calcutta and Delhi)

1. Pound together the prawns, onions, garlic, ginger and chillies into a coarse paste.
2. Wash and cut each brinjal into 4 sections, leaving the lower part near the stem uncut, a petal-like cup is thus formed to hold stuffing. Scoop out the seeds.
3. Mix pounded ingredients with turmeric, fish paste, and salt to taste. Stuff the brinjals.
4. Pour oil and enough water to cover. Keep on fire until brinjals are tender and the water is absorbed.

   Serves 4.

FRIED FISH WITH GINGER SAUCE (Siamese)

1 big fish (Pomfret of about 750 gm)
½ cup water
1 teaspoon salt
1 cup flour
1 tablespoon of olive oil
Frying fat or oil
Ginger sauce

1. Clean and dry fish with a clean cloth. With a sharp knife make deep incisions down to the bone diagonally across the fish to form little squares.
2. Mix the flour, salt and the olive oil thoroughly. Add the water to form a thick, smooth batter.
3. Have ready a deep pan of hot fat. Dip the fish in the batter. Fry till nearly browned. Drain well.
4. Pour the ginger sauce over the fish.
5. Garnish with parsley and chopped green chillies.
   Serves 4 to 6.

DEVILLED GRILLED FISH

250 gm good firm fillets (either pomfret or surmai)
1 teaspoon curry powder
1 tablespoon butter
A few drops of Worcester sauce
Salt and pepper

Spread the fish with butter, to which you have added a little curry powder and a few drops of Worcester sauce and grill.
Serves 4.

HON OF PRAWNS (Siamese)

About 1 cup of cream and milk of ½ a coconut
1 cup chopped fresh prawns
3 tablespoons of chopped spring onions
A little garlic (chopped)
Sugar, salt to taste
2 or 3 green chillies (chopped)
Tamarind pulp (imli) to taste

1. Boil the cream till it is oily. Add prawns and stir till well cooked, then add the milk, salt, sugar, spring onions, onion and chillies.
2. Boil until it is reduced to a creamy consistency. Add tamarind pulp.
3. Serve with raw vegetable salad (such as carrots, radish, cucumber and onion leeks) or fried vegetables.
   To be eaten with boiled rice.

SHRIMP TOAST (Thai)

6 slices stale bread (each piece divided into 4 squares)
1 cup ground shrimp
1 teaspoon finely chopped coriander
2 teaspoons finely chopped garlic
½ teaspoon salt
1 teaspoon soya sauce
1½ teaspoons pepper
1 egg, well beaten
4 cups oil (Postman oil)

1. Mix shrimp with coriander, garlic, soya sauce, stir and add egg, pepper.
2. Blend well and set aside.
3. Place one spoonful of the mixture onto each piece of bread. Deep fry with mixture down, until golden brown and crisp. Drain on paper towel and serve.
   Serves 6.

Paprika Chicken

1 or 2 young chickens

5 or 6 onions

Yolk of 1 or 2 eggs

1 cup of sour cream

1 tablespoon of paprika or mild red chilli powder

Salt and pepper

Cooking fat or butter

1. Slice the onions and cook in hot fat till a golden colour.
2. Add the chickens cut in quarters and sprinkle all with the paprika and, when the chickens are slightly coloured, add the yolks of eggs, well mixed with the sour cream. Season with salt and pepper and simmer till the chickens are quite tender. Rice is served with this dish.

Grilled Pork Chops with Orange Slices

1 pork chop for each person

1 good orange

A dash of brown sugar

Salt to taste

1. Season pork chops and brown on either side under hot grill.
2. Add thick slices of orange sprinkled with a little brown sugar and cook together until the chops are tender and the orange slices hot.
3. Serve with Worcester sauce, peas and creamed potatoes.

Chicken in Sour-Cream Gravy (Norway)

2 chickens, small fryers for frying
Salt and pepper
¼ lb butter
3 cups milk
2 tablespoons parsley (chopped)
¼ cup sherry
1 cup sour cream (yoghurt)

1. Season chicken with salt and pepper. Fry in butter until golden brown.
2. Place chicken and drippings into a casserole and cover with milk.
3. Cook very slowly for about 30 minutes until tender.
4. Add parsley and sherry and cook for 5-10 minutes more.
5. Add sour cream and stir into gravy.
6. Keep in oven for 5 more minutes. Serve.

Serves 4-6.

Garnish for Fish Preparations

(a) *Bananas and grapes*
Place alternate portions of fried potato straws, lightly fried sliced bananas and fried grapes round the fish.

(b) *Fried parsley*
Sprinkle fried parsley over and around the fried fish.

(c) *Rice*
Place tomato rice or cheese rice in the centre of the dish and surround with fish.

Mayonnaise, Ginger Sauce, Mint Sauce, Yogurt Sauce, Chocolate Sauce, Apple Sauce.

Water Melon Cocktail.

Open Egg Sandwich.

Burmese Coconut Blanc-Mange.

Banana Bread, Brown Bread.

Peach Melba.

Burmese Chicken Kauksewe

3½ lb chicken — 1 kg. 750 gm
2 quarts water — 8 cups
1 teaspoon turmeric (haldi)
10 onions
4 pods garlic
2 teaspoons dry giner or 1 piece green ginger
4 chillies or chilli powder
4 tablespoons of sesame (til) oil
3 cups coconut milk extracted (fresh)
1 cup of gram powder (besan)
3½ lb noodles or spaghetti

1. Cut the chicken in 4 pieces. Smear with turmeric powder and cook in 2 quarts water till tender. Put salt to taste. Cut meat from bones. Crack bones and add to stock, which continues to simmer to be strained later. Pound garlic and chillies together and rub over chicken. Heat oil in saucepan until smoking. Fry one sliced onion in oil. Add chicken and fry. Add stock and simmer.
2. Make a paste of gram powder and one cup water. Add the stock and cook 10 to 15 minutes. Pour coconut milk in last and boil for a few minutes longer. Add more salt if necessary.
3. Serve hot with noodles (Kauksewe).

   Serve 10.

   Accompaniments: Crisp fried straw potatoes, sliced hard-boiled eggs, fresh lime wedges (cut one into quarter) red chilli powder, coarsely cut spring onions.

Burmese Prawn Balachaung

7 oz dried prawns

11 oz sesame oil (til oil)

1½ oz shrimp paste (optional, it is available in Calcutta)

1 level teaspoon powdered turmeric

10 cloves garlic

1 medium-sized onion

1 inch fresh ginger

Salt to taste

3 chillies or more to taste may be ground and fried before adding prawns

1. Wash the prawns and grind or pound them in a mortar. Peel and slice very thin, the garlic, onion and ginger. Heat oil to fry garlic, onion and ginger, each in turn. Remove from oil and lay aside till required.
2. Add powdered turmeric and prawns to oil and fry till crisp. Strain through a strainer or colander, pouring oil into a spare container. In the oil that clings to the side of the pan, stir in the shrimp paste and stir until cooked, for 2 minutes or so. Now return the dried prawns that have been fried crisp to the pan and mix thoroughly with the shrimp paste. Add salt to taste. Garnish with fried garlic.
3. Serve with curry and rice or spread on bread.

Fish Mousse

250 gm of any good fish, shredded (available in India)

1 egg, well beaten

A little milk

¼ cup whipped cream

Beat the ingredients together and steam for two hours.

Serves 4.

Fish Kababs

1 kg firm fleshed fish (either surmai or pomfret)
2 cloves garlic
4 onions
½ cup yoghurt
Salt to taste
½ teaspoon ginger powder
1 teaspoon chilli powder
2 teaspoons garam masala
melted butter for basting

1. Cut the fish in cubes.
2. Chop the garlic very finely and add it to the bowl of water in which the fish is to be washed. Wash and drain the fish cubes.
3. Chop the onions finely and mix with the yoghurt, salt and spices.
4. Marinate the fish in it for 2 hours.
5. Thread the fish on to skewers and grill.
6. Brush with melted butter while grilling.
7. Button mushrooms can be included, if liked.
   Serves 10-12.

Creamy Lemon Chicken (Italy)

1 young chicken
1 tablespoon butter
1 glass sherry
2 egg yolks
½ pint cream
1 cup grated lemon rind

1. Divide the chicken into several pieces.
2. Melt the butter in a pan, pour in the sherry and add the pieces of chicken.
3. Beat the egg yolks with the cream and pour over the chicken and heat, stirring, until it has only slightly thickened, sprinkle with grated lemon rind.
4. The sauce will thicken as it cools, serve cold.

West African Groundnut Stew

1 young chicken

1 kg groundnuts (peanuts)

1 tablespoon flour

1 onion, chopped and fried

6 hardboiled eggs

1. Boil the chicken gently in water to cover, when cooked place on one side, keeping the stock.
2. Place groundnuts on a flat pan in a low oven to brown slowly. Remove skins when brown, crush nuts with a rolling pin until a smooth pulp is obtained.
3. Turn into a mixture bowl with about half of the chicken stock and stir well. Blend the flour with a little stock and mix in with stock in bowl.
4. Cut chicken into portions and place in a casserole with the fried onion. Pour on stock with groundnut pulp added; if chicken pieces are not covered, add some of the plain stock. Add red peppers, close casserole, place in a moderate oven and cook for about 30 minutes until ready to serve.
5. Place eggs either halved or whole, into the stew 15 minutes before serving.
6. Let your friends help themselves to rice, heaped on to their plates, then pour the stew over it, sprinkling on the accompaniments.
7. Fruit salad as a sweet afterwards is a refreshing and adequate finale.

   Accompaniments – Boiled rice, carrots, mango chutney, shredded coconut, groundnuts, finely chopped chillies, bananas (sliced), tomatoes (sliced), according to what is easily available.

An eating-house keeper doesn't care how big your appetite is.

BAHMI (A Chinese dish popular in Indonesia)

250 gm vermicelli (Chinese vermicelli available in Delhi)

Salt to taste

2 or 3 large onions chopped

2 cloves of garlic, crushed

Oil or fat for frying

250 gm pork (available in Delhi)

500 gm mixed vegetables – cauliflower, cabbage, French beans

250 gm spring onions

2 heads of celery

1 cup fresh prawns, shelled

An omelette made from 2 eggs

1. Boil the vermicelli in ample salted water for 10 minutes. Fry onion and garlic in oil until golden-brown. Remove from pan and keep warm.
2. Fry the pork until tender in same oil. Meanwhile, prepare vegetables and cut into small pieces. Boil in water until half cooked. Drain.
3. When meat is tender, cut into small pieces and put into a large saucepan.
4. Add all vegetables, vermicelli and prawns, heat together for 10 minutes.
5. Serve the Bahmi in a shallow dish and put strips of omelette (arranged on top of the vermicelli in lattice style, as in tarts).

   Accompaniments – Soya sauce and side dishes of tomato, cucumber, cut lengthwise into 3 in strips, any salad leaves, lemon wedges.

   Serves 4.

FRIED SPRING CHICKEN

2 spring chickens
Salt
½ cup flour
½ cup thin cream
Parsley or celery
2 cups fat or oil for frying

1. Cut the chicken in half. Season with salt and chilli powder, dredge with flour.
2. Melt the fat, brown the chickens on each side quickly, leave to cook more slowly in the same pan for 30 minutes.
3. Thicken the fat in the pan with flour. Add the cream gradually to make thick gravy.
4. Serve garnished with parsley.
   Serves 4-6.

CREAMED CHICKEN

2 cups cooked chicken
2 tablespoons butter
2 tablespoons flour
1 cup milk or cream
Salt and pepper
1 tablespoon parsley
1 egg yolk

Make a white sauce of the butter, flour and milk. Season with salt and pepper. Add the parsley and chicken and cook until the sauce is thoroughly hot again. Beat the egg yolk, adding two tablespoons of milk, and pour into the mixture. Cook for two minutes, stirring constantly, and serve in a border of riced potatoes. (*See recipe for riced potatoes under Vegetarian section.*)
Serves 3 to 4.

Spaghetti Bolognese

1 onion
1 carrot
1 stick celery
2 tablespoons oil
12 tomatoes
200 gm spaghetti
1 cup minced meat
2 tablespoons butter
Salt and pepper
Some red chilli powder (if liked)
1 cup grated cheese or more if needed

1. Fry chopped onion, carrot and celery in oil and butter for 5 minutes, then add the mince and the skinned tomatoes. Season to taste and simmer for 30 minutes.
2. Cook spaghetti in boiling salted water for 20 minutes.
3. Drain and place in serving dish, pour on meat mixture and serve very hot, topped with plenty of grated cheese.
4. Serve also chunks of French bread and butter.
   Serves 6 to 8.

Mutton Chops

6 mutton chops
Oil
Salt and pepper

1. Mutton chops should be not less than one inch thick.
2. The best way to cook them is to broil them.
3. Sprinkle with salt and pepper, oil both sides and broil on charcoal fire turning very often.
4. Serve them on hot dish, with French fried potatoes and sprigs of parsley.
   Serves 3.

Fish Baked in Banana Leaves (Indonesian)

500 gm fish (pomfret or surmai)
4 red chillies (seeds removed)
1 inch fresh ginger
1 clove garlic
l large onion
1 teaspoon turmeric powder (haldi)
2 teaspoons lemon juice
Salt to taste
1 teaspoon sugar

1. Cut the fish in slices and rub with salt.
2. Grind the ginger, chillies, garlic and onion, add the sugar and turmeric and mix to a paste with lemon juice.
3. Spread the mixture over the fish slices, wrap them in banana leaves and bake in a slow oven for about one hour or steam for about 20 minutes or more.
   Serves 6 to 8.

Chinese Fried Fish Chinois

½ kg butter fish or any kind of meaty fish
1 tablespoon cornflour
¾ teaspoon salt
3 tablespoons cooking oil

1. Wash and cut fish in thin slices 1½ inches long and dredge with cornflour.
2. On very hot fire, heat the oil in a preheated frying pan. Drop fish in pan, sprinkle with salt, as one side browns turn fish carefully so as not to break the thin slice of fish.
3. Put in serving dish at once.
   Serves 4.

Pineapple with Meat or with Veal (A Danish way)

6 small, thin fillets of veal

250 gm mushrooms, sliced (available in Delhi)

Butter for frying

6 pineapple slices

1 cupful cream

1. Fry the meat and mushrooms in the butter. Lift out and drain.
2. Put the fillets on a hot dish, keep mushrooms warm.
3. Gently heat the pineapple slices in the pan, put one on each of the fillets, pile mushrooms in centre of rings.
4. Add cream to the juice left in the pan, heat very gently. Pour over meat and pineapple and serve at once.

Serves 4 to 6.

Cubes of Mutton in Batter (Malayan)

500 gm mutton from the leg or shoulder

1 teaspoon chilli powder

1 stick cinnamon (about 1 inch)

Salt

1 teaspoon aniseed (saunf)

1 cup flour

1 egg

½ cup water

Fat for frying

1. Cut the meat into cubes and place in a saucepan together with the chilli powder and salt. Cover with little water and simmer until the meat is tender and dry. Remove from pan.
2. Mix flour with egg and water into a batter and add aniseed. Dip mutton pieces in this batter and fry in deep fat.

Serves 4 to 6.

Fish Fritters

½ kg good white fish
3 eggs
3 tablespoons flour
Salt and pepper
Minced garlic (3 cloves)
Minced parsley (1 teaspoon)
2 green chillies (chopped) if liked

1. Cook the fish and mash them.
2. Beat the yolks of the eggs until light and thick, then add, little by little, the flour, salt, pepper, the minced garlic and parsley, and the fish.
3. Lastly add the whites of the eggs beaten to a froth.
4. Drop spoonfuls of this mixture into hot fat and fry to a golden brown.

Poulet a la Creole (The French West Indies)

A young chicken
Some butter
2 onions (sliced)
A little saffron (kesar)
1 tablespoon curry powder
Chilli powder and salt
A little coconut milk

1. Joint the chicken.
2. Brown the pieces of chicken in hot butter and, when well browned, add 2 sliced onions, which have also been browned in butter.
3. Season with a little saffron, curry powder, chilli powder and salt.
4. Simmer till the chicken is tender, and a few minutes before serving add a little coconut milk and stir well.
5. Plain boiled rice is served with.

Note: You can cook either fish or mutton in the same way.

A Jam Panggang (Indonesia)

1 chicken

Small piece ginger

1 small piece saffron (kesar)

1 clove garlic

2 medium-sized onions

6 chillies or less to taste

Milk of 1 coconut

Small piece lemon grass (available in Delhi)

1. Split chicken along breast.
2. Grind spices with garlic and onions, mix with coconut milk.
3. Add lemon grass. Bring to boil in pan.
4. Put chicken in pan, stirring liquid and turning.
5. Boil slowly until all milk is evaporated from the frying pan.
6. Remove chicken from pan and brown over a charcoal fire.
7. Serve with plain rice and any salad.

Hawaiian Chops

4 rib chops or pork chops (3/4 inch thick)

Salt, pepper and a dash of Aji-no-moto

4 slices pineapple

4 dried prunes

8 medium-sized carrots

½ cup hot water

1. Brown chops in hot fat, season.
2. Place pineapple on each chop, with prune in centre of slice.
3. Arrange carrots around chops.
4. Add water, cover and cook slowly until the chops are tender.

Lamb Chops (Fried) with Cheese and Macaroni

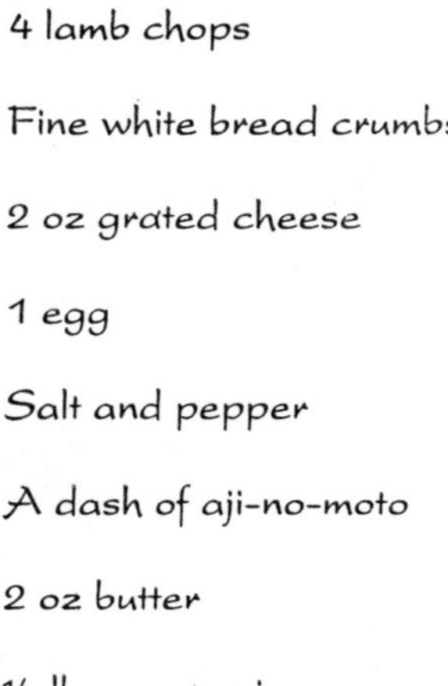
4 lamb chops

Fine white bread crumbs

2 oz grated cheese

1 egg

Salt and pepper

A dash of aji-no-moto

2 oz butter

¼ lb macaroni

Postman oil for frying

1. Mix a good sprinkling of salt, pepper and Aji-no-moto with the bread crumbs and 1 oz of grated cheese.

2. Make the butter hot, and brush each chop well over with it.

3. Dip in well beaten egg and then in the seasoned bread-crumbs, and fry a golden brown in hot fat.

4. Drain well and serve in a border of boiled macaroni, sprinkled with a remainder of the cheese.

5. Enough for 4 persons.

Scrambled Fish

4 oz cooked fish

4 eggs

2 oz butter

2 tablespoons milk

Salt and pepper

4 slices buttered toast

Little mustard

1. Beat the eggs just enough to mix white and yolk, season them with salt, pepper and, if liked, a little more mustard. Mix the milk with them.
2. Flake the fish and remove any skin or bones.
3. Add it to the eggs.
4. Melt the butter in a saucepan, turn in the mixture and stir over very gentle heat until it thickens.
5. Serve very hot piled on squares of hot buttered toast.

EGGS

Eggs can be cooked in very elaborate ways, but they are also an excellent base for quickly cooked, simple yet substantial dishes which, although quick and easy to make, contain the essential elements for a well balanced meal and will give you an endless variety.

Eggs are a versatile food and can be used in the following ways:

1. *In icing cakes and also in making cakes*

a) *Seven minute icing*

1 unbeaten egg-white
1/4 cup granulated sugar
3 tablespoons cold water
1/2 teaspoon flavouring extract

Place all the ingredients in a double boiler. Place over boiling water and beat with an egg-beater for seven minutes. Add flavouring, beat, and spread on cake.

b) *Chocolate icing*: Add to the above 1 ½ ounces melted unsweetened chocolate two minutes before removing from fire.

c) *Coffee icing*: Use cold boiled coffee instead of water.

2. *To thicken cream*:
Whisk the whites of egg with some sugar till very stiff and add a little juice of lime and then mix with the cream.

3. *In souffles of a) old and hot puddings*
b) fish, chicken, cheese and spinach dishes

4. *See recipe of Floating Island for steam white egg balls in hot milk.*

5. *In meringues for puddings*

2 egg whites
1/8 teaspoon cream of tartar with a dash of salt
½ cup sugar
½ teaspoon vanilla essence

Beat egg whites with cream of tartar and salt until stiff but not dry. Add sugar, 1 tablespoon at a time, beating until stiff after each addition. Fold in the vanilla essence. Heap in rounds onto baking sheet covered with heavy ungreased paper.

Bake in a slow oven (275ºF) for 40 to 60 minutes or until lightly browned.

Remove at once from paper.

Makes 18 large meringues.

Add ½ cup finely chopped and roasted peanuts to the mixture if liked.

b) *Meringues with cream for tea*

The same mixture as above. Drop it onto a buttered sheet in small heaps. Then bake the same way.

Remove carefully from the baking sheet, and when cold sandwich them together in pairs with whipped cream and powdered sugar.

6. *With whites of eggs for breakfast*

See Fluffy Egg recipe on page 69

6. *Egg drinks for invalids*

a) *Albumen water I*

The white of 1 egg
1 cup ice-water
Sugar to taste
1 tablespoon lemon-juice

Stir the white of an egg with a silver fork, and add the water. Serve plain or sweeten and flavour with lemon juice. Mix well.

b) *Albumen water II*

2 teaspoons sugar
½ cup warm water
2 tablespoons lemon-juice
3 tablespoons orange-juice
1 egg-white
Pinch of salt
Crushed ice

Dissolve the sugar in the warm water, add lemon juice. Beat egg white enough so that it will mix; add salt and put in with remaining ingredients.

Shake or beat the mixture. Strain and serve with crushed ice.

Baked Eggs with Cream and Toast

1-2 slices of bread per person

Yoghurt or fresh cream (1 tablespoon)

1 egg for each piece of bread

Salt and pepper

1. Cut as many thick slices of bread as required, that is one or two slices per person. Toast these on both sides. Trim or cut them with a cutter until they are round, then cut out a hole in the centre of each piece leaving at least an inch of bread all round.
2. Put the rings into a flat baking dish and gradually pour yoghurt or fresh cream over them. Let the cream be absorbed but do not let the bread become soggy.
3. Break an egg into each hole, sprinkle lightly with salt and pepper and a film of cream over each egg and bake until the eggs are set but not hard.
4. Fried tomatoes, sauted potatoes or fresh mushrooms may be served with this dish.

   Serves 1.

Hurry-up Curried Eggs

6 hard boiled eggs

1 cup mayonnaise

2 teaspoons curry powder

1 cup cooked rice

Salt and pepper to taste

1. Cut a slice off the wide end of 6 hardboiled eggs. Stand eggs on platter.
2. Top with mayonnaise and mix with 2 teaspoons curry powder.
3. Serve with rice and sliced tomatoes.

   Serves 6.

Surprise Eggs

6 eggs
12 rounds brown bread and butter
For the filling
½ cup finely chopped cooked mushrooms
1 cup cooked ham (minced or chopped)
Salt, pepper and any other seasoning according to your preference
Tomatoes to garnish

1. Hardboil and halve the eggs.
2. Cut small thin slices off the bottom to make them stand and remove the yolks.
3. Make a puree of the ham, mix with egg yolks and chopped mushrooms and seasoning.
4. Fill egg cases with the mixture.
5 Garnish with tomatoes

Serves 6.

Fluffy Egg

1 egg per person
1 slice toast
Salt and pepper
Grated cheese or slice of ham

Butter the toast and cover it with the grated cheese or a slice of ham. Arrange the stiffly beaten egg-white on the toast. Leave a hole in the middle, slide the egg yolk into the hole. Sprinkle with salt and pepper. Cook in a very hot oven until the white is golden and the yolk is set.
Serves 1.

Swiss Eggs

3 eggs
2 tablespoons butter
½ cup grated cheese
1 tablespoonful cream
Salt and cayenne (optional, use a little red chilli powder instead)

1. Sprinkle half the grated cheese into a greased fireproof dish.
2. Break the eggs on top of the cheese, keeping them whole.
3. Pour the cream over the eggs and sprinkle the remainder of the cheese on top. Season with salt and pepper.
4. Bake in a moderate oven until eggs are set.
   Serves 3.

Sweet Potato Croquettes

2½ cups mashed sweet potatoes
1½ tablespoons butter
Salt and pepper
2 tablespoons sugar
½ cup crumbs
2 eggs

Combine sweet potatoes, butter, salt, pepper and sugar. Beat until fluffy. Chill. Shape, roll in crumbs, then in egg and again in crumbs. Fry in hot deep fat for 3 to 5 minutes. Drain. Makes 6 croquettes.
Serves 3.

Fried Egg Fingers

2 eggs
2 slices of bread
Fat or butter for frying
Salt and pepper to taste

1. Beat eggs, season well and pour into a shallow dish.
2. Cut fingers of bread and remove crusts.
3. Soak in the egg until this is quite absorbed. Lift off fingers carefully into hot fat and fry.
4. This often appeals to people who do not like ordinary fried eggs.
   Serves 2.

Cheese Scrambled Eggs

6 eggs
$^1/_3$ cup cream
¾ teaspoon salt
A dash of pepper
2 tablespoons fat or butter (melted)
½ cup shredded cheese
2 tablespoons chopped green onion leeks

1. Mix 6 beaten eggs with $^1/_3$ cup light cream, ¾ teaspoon salt and a dash of pepper. Melt 2 tablespoons fat in a skillet, add eggs.
2. Cook, stirring frequently till eggs begin to set and then sprinkle with the shredded cheese.
3. Continue cooking till eggs are just firm and the cheese melts.
4. Trim with 2 tablespoons chopped green onion tops.
   Makes 6 servings.

French Toast

2 eggs, well beaten
1 cup milk
6-8 slices of old bread
1 teaspoon salt
3 teaspoons sugar
¾ teaspoon nutmeg (jaiphal)
¼ teaspoon cinnamon
1 tablespoon flour
Butter or ghee

1. Mix together all ingredients except the bread.
2. After mixing thoroughly, dip both sides of the bread into the batter.
3. Fry in a hot pan in a small amount of butter or ghee.
4. Serve with sugar or jam.

   Serves 6.

Eggs in Nests

Cut rounds off bread 1 to 2 inches thick. Scoop a hole on one side and fry the bread, hole downwards. Turn and break an egg into the hole and fry. Garnish with grated cheese and serve.

Cheese Toast (French)

2 eggs
1½ tablespoons cream
1½ tablespoons flour
1 cup grated cheese (use Amul cheese)
Salt and pepper
4 slices of bread

1. Mix all ingredients, except the bread, well together and work the mixture until firm.
2. Spread this mixture on slices of bread about ½ inch thick.
3. Fry in deep fat putting the cheese side down first, then turn over.
4. Remove when the toast is golden brown, and cut one slice of toast into 4 squares. This dish is quickly made, delicious and not expensive.
Serves 4.

Cheese Straws

250 gm Amul cheese
250 gm flour
1 cup fresh butter
1 yolk of egg
¼ cup milk

Cut butter into small pieces, rub with flour and work in the cheese and milk till you get a paste. Put aside for half an hour. Then roll out to a thickness of ¼ inch, cut into strips and put on a lightly buttered baking tin – bake for 14 minutes in a moderately hot oven.

Burmese Egg Dish

4 eggs

250 gm rice

Salt

125 gm mushrooms, sliced

4 small sausages

About ½ cup fat for frying

½ cup fresh or tinned prawns

½ cupful cooked green peas

1. Cook the rice in salted water for 15-20 minutes. Drain and dry in the oven.
2. Fry mushrooms and sausages and the prawns in a little fat. Slice the sausages.
3. Then fry the rice in 1 cup fat. Mix the mushrooms, sausages, prawns and rice together, and peas and heat thoroughly. Turn on to a dish and keep warm.
4. Meanwhile fry the eggs and place on top of the dish.

Serves 4.

Milk Toast (USA)

6 slices buttered toast

2 tablespoons flour

2 tablespoons butter

2 cups hot milk

Salt

Make a white sauce of the flour, butter, milk and salt and pour it over the buttered toast and serve immediately.

Serves 6.

RICE

Coconut Rice (Burmese)

5 cups (2½ lb) rice
2 coconuts
2 tablespoons oil
1 teaspoon sugar
¼ teaspoon salt
2 onions (chopped)
One pinch turmeric powder

1. Grate the flesh of 2 coconuts and place in a muslin bag over a bowl. Pour hot water over the coconut and squeeze out the milk. Repeat till all the milk has been extracted.
2. Heat the oil in a saucepan and fry the onions, but do not brown, add rice and fry for a few minutes.
3. Cover the rice with coconut milk. The milk should stand about one inch over the rice. Season with salt, sugar and a pinch of turmeric powder. Stir till well mixed. Cook till the milk is evaporated and the rice tender.
4. If there is not enough milk add water to make up the amount of liquid required.
5. Serve with good chicken curry.

Serves 10-12.

Cheese Rice

1 cup good cooked rice
1 clove garlic (chopped)
1 small piece of fresh ginger (chopped and crushed)
250 gm good tomatoes (chopped)
2 onions (chopped)
2 tablespoons oil
1 cup grated cheese
¼ teaspoon cayenne pepper (if not available use mild chilli powder)
Salt to taste

1. Heat oil in a saucepan and fry the onions until golden brown. Take the onions out and keep aside.
2. In the same oil, cook garlic, ginger, chilli powder and tomatoes until the tomatoes are soft.
3. To the tomato puree, add rice and the grated cheese and cook for a few minutes till the cheese melts.
4. Garnish with fried onions. Serve with fried fish.

SAVOURY STEAMED RICE (Chinese)

8 oz good rice
4 oz chicken meat
4 oz. lamb
1 piece of celery
6 pieces of fresh mushrooms (available in Delhi)
½ teaspoon Aji-no-moto
2 tablespoons soya sauce
1 teaspoon cornflour
Salt to taste

1. Cut chicken and lamb into pieces and slice vegetables.
2. Season with salt and Aji-no-moto, soya sauce and cornflour.
3. Put on top of rice which has been prepared for steaming up to boiling stage.
4. Turn heat to low and simmer for 25 minutes. The steam will tenderise the meats and all the flavour will be absorbed by the rice.

Anchovy Rice

3 cups boiled and drained rice

1 level teaspoonful curry powder

3 teaspoonful anchovy sauce

2 beaten egg-yolks

A dash of chilli powder

Mix lightly together with a fork three breakfast cupfuls of boiled and drained rice, a level teaspoonful of curry powder, three teaspoonfuls of anchovy sauce, two beaten egg-yolks and little chilli powder to taste. Heat through to cook the egg slightly and serve.

Serves 8.

Golden Rice

2 onions (chopped)

¼ cup hutter

250 gm rice

3 cups boiling water

Some grated cheese

Salt and pepper

A little melted butter

1. Fry two chopped onions in ¼ cup of butter and 250 gm of rice and go on frying until the rice is golden brown.
2. Then add 3 cups of boiling water, season with salt and pepper and cook for about half an hour until the rice is tender.
3. Serve sprinkled with grated cheese and melted butter and bake until golden brown on top of the dish in a hot oven or under the grill.

   Fried or grilled mushrooms are good with this.

   Serves 4.

FRIED RICE (Chinese) I

3 cups cold cooked rice
2 eggs
Spring onions, chopped
1 tablespoon oil
2 teaspoons soya sauce
Salt to taste

1. Heat oil in a frying-pan, add beaten eggs seasoned with salt and stir briskly until nearly set. Add the cold rice and mix well. Add soya sauce and chopped spring onions and stir until rice is thoroughly heated. Serve.
2. Chopped fried bacon, cooked ham can be added to the rice.

FRIED RICE (Chinese) II

2 tablespoons oil
2 cups onions (coarsely chopped)
2 cups cold cooked rice
2 eggs
1 tablespoon soya sauce
½ teaspoon salt and a dash of Aji-no-moto
2 cups chopped cooked chicken, ham or chopped peanuts

1. Heat pan, add 2 tablespoons oil and fry 2 cups onion, coarsely chopped until brown. Add 2 cups cold cooked rice and saute.
2. Add a mixture of 2 eggs, stirred slightly, 1 tablespoon soya sauce and half teaspoon salt and Aji-no-moto, saute until done.
3. For variety add 2 cups chopped cooked chicken, ham or green peppers, chopped or peanuts (shelled and roasted).
4. Heat thoroughly.

Serves 4-6.

Kedgere

2 cups flaked cooked fish (surmai or one bone fish)
1 cup cooked rice
2 hard-boiled eggs
4 tablespoons butter
Salt and pepper

Heat fish, rice and chopped egg white in butter. Season and sprinkle with sieved egg yolks.
Serves 4.

Malayan Fried Balls of Rice

½ cup rice, boiled in the usual way
1 tomato, skinned
1 small onion, chopped finely
½ beaten egg to bind
A dash of Aji-no-moto
Egg and bread crumbs to coat
A deep pan of oil for frying
Absorbent paper for draining

1. Boil the rice until it is soft and dry.
2. Place the tomato in a small basin and pour boiling water over it, leave in the water for 3 minutes and then take off the skin with a vegetable knife. Prepare and chop the onion.
3. Lightly fry the tomato and onion together and then put them into the rice. Add sufficient well-beaten egg to bind the mixture together with a dash of Aji-no-moto; stirring it with a wooden spoon over a very low fire.
4. Turn the rice mixture onto a plate, cover and leave it to cool.
5. Divide the cooled mixture into equal sized pieces and roll them into halls about the size of walnuts.
6. Coat the balls of rice with beaten egg and browned bread crumbs, and fry in a deep or shallow pan of oil until they are golden brown. Drain on absorbent paper and serve with a chilli sauce.

RICE MILAN STYLE

500 gm rice

1 small chopped onion

8 cups boiling stock

¼ teaspoon saffron previously soaked (kesar)

½ cup butter

Salt and pepper

About 1 cup grated cheese

1. Heat the butter in a large saucepan, add the onion and when it starts to brown throw in the rice, stirring all the while to prevent sticking.
2. When the rice is transparent add the stock, salt, pepper and the saffron. Mix these ingredients well in the pan and cook over a simmering flame until the rice has absorbed all the liquid.
3. Taste before serving, add the cheese and a knob of butter. When this has melted, serve the rice as hot as possible.

   Serves 8.

Nasigoreng – Fried Rice (Indonesian)

1½ cups oil

8 small onions (sliced fine)

4 fresh green or red chillies (sliced fine)

¼ cup each of diced fresh prawns, ham, cooked pork or chicken, and mushrooms

4 cups cold boiled rice

1 teaspoon soya sauce and a little salt to taste

4 beaten eggs

1 cup spring onions (chopped)

2 stalks celery (chopped)

1. Put 1 ½ cup oil into pan. When hot fry 8 onions and 4 chillies; when soft, add ¼ cup each of diced fresh prawns, ham, cooked pork or chicken, and mushrooms.
2. Stir in 4 cups cold boiled rice, adding a teaspoonful soya sauce and salt to taste.
3. Add 4 beaten eggs and stir well till egg is cooked and rice is dry. Add chopped spring onion and celery.
4. Serve on hot platter.

   Serves 8 to 10.

Buttered Rice

1. Cook the rice in the usual way, drain it well and dry it.
2. Now in a hot pan stir a little butter and a well beaten egg with a spoonful of chopped parsley and cook just enough for the egg to set lightly. Stir with a fork before serving.

Almond Rice

3 cups hot cooked rice

½ cup coarsely chopped almonds

6 tablespoons butter

2 tablespoons Worcester sauce

A dash of Aji-no-moto

A dash of paprika (or mild chilli powder)

1. Melt butter and stir in the Worcester sauce.
2. Add nuts, and brown them.
3. Mix well together with the hot rice with Aji-no-moto and a dash of paprika powder.
4. Serve hot with fried chops and fried chicken.

Rice Border

1 cup rice

3 cups white stock

1 tablespoon salt

3 egg-yolks

2 tablespoons butter or any other fat

3 tablespoons milk or cream

1. Cook washed rice in white stock for ½ hour, then add salt and butter or other fat and cook slowly 20 minutes more.
2. Beat the yolks of the eggs with the cream or milk and stir in.
3. Grease a border mold, pack the rice firmly into it, let it stand about ten minutes in a warm place and turn it out on a hot platter.
4. Fill the centre with any meat or chicken preparations.

VEGETARIAN RECIPES

Even those of you who are not vegetarian will enjoy trying out these recipes, and will find them useful on a number of occasions when meatless dishes are required

Stuffed Onions

4 large onions
1 cup grated cheese
1 cup grated carrots
½ cup chopped walnuts
4 tablespoons cream
Salt and pepper

1. Cook the onions in salted water for ½ - ¾ hour, scoop out the centres and chop them.
2. Mix the grated carrots, 1 cup cheese and the chopped walnuts with the chopped onions and the cream. Season to taste.
3. Fill the onion shells with the mixture, sprinkle the remaining cheese on top and bake in a moderate oven for about 30 minutes.
   Serve with parsley sauce.
   Serves 4.

Creamy Jacket Potatoes

5-6 potatoes

½ cup butter

2 egg yolks

4 tablespoons cream

Salt, pepper and nutmeg (jaiphal)

½ cup grated cheese

Parsley or celery

1. Prick each potato, after scrubbing it well, and bake slowly till soft.
2. Cut a hole in each and remove the inside carefully using a small spoon, so as not to break the potato case.
3. Sieve the potato, and mix with a generous amount of butter, the egg yolks and the cream.
4. Season, add grated nutmeg to taste and return the mixture to the potato cases.
5. Sprinkle with cheese, dot with shavings of butter and bake in a moderate oven till golden on top.
6. Garnish with parsley.

Serves 6.

Potato with Baked Eggs

4 lb (2 kg) cooked potatoes
½ cup butter
6 eggs
4 tablespoons milk
Salt and pepper
1 beaten egg to glaze
½ cup grated cheese

1. Sieve the potatoes.
2. Add the butter, 2 eggs, milk and seasonings, and mix well together.
3. Pipe the potato into a fireproof dish (or pie-dish), leaving four hollows.
4. Put one of the eggs in each hollow, and sprinkle with cheese.
5. Glaze the potato with the beaten egg, and bake till the eggs are set and the cheese lightly browned.
   Serves 4.

Cream Potatoes

2 cups diced cold cooked potatoes
1½ cups white sauce
Salt and pepper

Combine potatoes and white sauce and beat thoroughly. Season with salt and pepper.

OR

Use milk instead of white sauce. Dice potatoes into a skillet in which 2 tablespoons butter has been melted. Season with salt and pepper and almost cover with milk. Simmer, uncovered until milk is absorbed, tilting pan occasionally and basting top of potatoes with milk.

Burmese Pickle (Thanai)

Any vegetables in season

Cabbage, cauliflower, carrots, capsicum, radish, brinjal and green chillies.

500 gm of all mixed vegetables

3 tablespoons vinegar

6 large onions

½ cup til oil

2 tablespoons black or white til seeds

1 teaspoon salt

1. Any vegetables in season. Boil in a little vinegar and water (do not boil too soft) allow to cool, then take out of water and squeeze well.
2. Slice up some onions – cook the oil, put in onions and fry.
3. Cook the *til* seeds just put them in a dry frying pan on the stove for about 5 minutes, until they begin to pop up.
4. Mix the vegetables, fried onions and *til* seeds together with a little salt and taste.

CARROTS contain sugar and are rich in mineral salts and vitamins A and C. They also contain carotene which is claimed to be beneficial to the eyesight and was part of the daily diet of night pilots of the Royal Air Force. Dieticians insist that carrots should be eaten raw.

Sweet Corn Toast

1 cupful of drained tinned corn
1 teaspoonful chopped onion
1½ tablespoons butter
¼ cup cream
Salt and chilli powder to taste
4 slices of buttered toast

1. Rather good for a quick snackish meal. Cook a teaspoonful of chopped onion in a level tablespoonful and a half of butter for 2 or 3 minutes, stirring all the time, then add a breakfast cupful of drained tinned corn, chopped if you like, some thin cream or creamy milk and seasoning of salt and mild chilli powder.
2. Bring to the boil, simmer for 5 minutes then pour over slices of butter toasts and serve at once.
Serves 4.

Brinjal Bartha

3 or 4 brinjals
2 onions
2 green chillies
¼ cup thick coconut milk
½ teaspoon mustard or olive oil
1 lemon juice
Salt to taste

Boil and bake the brinjals, skin and then pulp them with very finely minced onions, chopped green or red chillies, a little thick coconut milk and less than ½ teaspoonful of mustard or olive oil and salt and lemon juice to taste.
Serves 4.

SPINACH ROLLS

250 gm spinach
1 cup white sauce
1 slice bread
2 tablespoons butter
1 cup milk
2 eggs
½ cup grated cheese
Salt and pepper

1. Wash the spinach, reserve 8 large leaves. Cook the rest, drain and chop. Mix with the white sauce, season with salt and pepper.
2. Cut bread into small slices and fry quickly in the butter. Mix with the spinach mixture.
3. Spread the mixture on the blanched spinach leaves, roll and arrange in a shallow fireproof dish.
4. Beat the eggs with the milk, cook slowly until the mixture thickens and stir in the grated cheese.
5. Pour over the spinach rolls. Bake in a moderate oven for 20 minutes.
   Serves 4.

SPINACH is rich in vitamins and mineral salts. Much of these valuable properties are lost by prolonged cooking, and for this reason, dieticians urge that the young spinach leaves should be eaten raw in salad.

Aubergine Caviar (Russian)

2 medium-sized aubergines (brinjals)
1 onion
2 tablespoons olive oil (or salad oil)
Pepper and salt to taste
Juice of 1 lemon
2 tablespoons bottled tomato sauce
1 tablespoonful Worcester sauce

1. Bake the aubergines in a moderate oven until they are soft. Peel them and chop finely. Chop the onion finely and fry in oil until soft. Add the aubergine, mixing and stirring until it is smooth. Season with salt and pepper, lemon juice and the sauces. Mix well together and continue cooking over a low heat until it is a smooth paste.
2. Serve cold with thin slices of rye-bread and butter or brown bread and butter or toasted buttered bread. It is served in small containers sunk in powdered ice, decorated with tiny sprigs of parsley.
3. It is nice to serve with *puri* or *paratha* in India.

Cream Cheese

4 cups milk
Juice of 1 lemon
Cream and salt

1. Boil the milk and add lemon juice.
2. Stir and when the milk curdles take off the fire.
3. Strain into a piece of muslin or thin cloth but keep the whey.
4. Hang the cheese till all the water has dripped off.
5. Moisten curd with cream and salt and chill.

Green Capsicum Rounds

10 to 12 capsicums
2 cups cream cheese
½ cup grated cheese
1 tablespoon grated onion
1 teaspoon salt
½ cup toasted chopped walnuts
½ cup diced red pepper
Parsley sprigs or celery (for garnish)

1. Cut off tops of peppers (capsicum), remove and discard ribs and seeds.
2. In small bowl with electric mixer, beat cheese with onion and salt until smooth and well blended – stir in walnuts and red pepper.
3. Using a teaspoon, put cheese mixture into peppers. Chill for at least 2 hours.
4. Cut in ½ inch crosswise slices to serve.
5. Garnish with parsley on the pepper.

Serves 10-12.

Potato Pancakes

2 eggs, slightly beaten
2 tablespoons flour
l to ½ teaspoons salt
1 tablespoon butter (melted)
2 tablespoons butter (melted)
2 tablespoons milk
3 to 4 medium potatoes (grated)

Combine eggs, flour, salt, butter, grated potatoes and milk. Drop by spoonfuls on a well buttered *tawa* or a griddle. Bake until golden brown on both sides. Make 12 to 14 pancakes.

Serves 6-8.

Burmese Balachaung.

Fried Fish with Ginger Sauce.

Creamy Jacket Potatoes.

Aubergine Caviar (Brinjal) Russian.

Sweet and Sour *Paneer* with Sprouted Dal.

Cheese Sticks.

Cheese and Orange Marmalade with Brown Bread.

Sandwiches.

Belgian Cucumber

4 medium-sized cucumbers

2 egg yolks

1 cup yoghurt

1 cup mayonnaise

2 teaspoons chopped parsley

1. Peel 4 medium-sized cucumbers and cut them into rounds about 2 inches thick.
2. Cook in fast boiling salted water until tender (about 10 minutes).
3. Drain well and arrange in a fireproof dish.
4. Beat 2 egg yolks, mix with 1 cup of yoghurt and 1 cup of mayonnaise, and warm gently, but do not boil.
5. Pour this mixture over the cucumbers, sprinkle with chopped parsley and serve with thin brown bread and butter.
   Serves 6-8.

Serbian Cabbage (Belgrade)

1 (3 pounds) shredded cabbage

2 cups of milk (1 can evaporated milk if available)

1 cup dry bread crumbs

½ cup butter or margarine

6-8 slices of ham

8-12 boiled medium potatoes

1. Place cabbage in a shallow 4 quart casserole (or any pie-dish).
2. Pour milk over, sprinkle with bread crumbs and dot with butter.
3. Cover, bake for 30 minutes or until crumbs are lightly browned and cabbage is tender.
4. Serve with ham slices on one side, cabbage in the middle and few potatoes on either side.
   Serves 6-8.

Roast Pumpkin

1 kg pumpkin

1 cup oil or dripping

1. Remove the skin from the pumpkin, scoop out the seeds and throw them away.
2. Cut into large chunks, place around the meat or in a roasting tin containing about 1 cup oil or dripping.
3. Spoon the dripping over the pumpkin and roast till golden brown and crisp.

Onion Bhaji

500 gm onion
¼ teaspoon turmeric
1 teaspoon chilli powder
1 teaspoon garam masala
Salt to taste
A few coriander leaves (optional)

1. Slice the onions thickly.
2. Heat the ghee and add the onion, turmeric, chilli, garam masala and salt and fry for 3 or 4 minutes, over brisk fire.
3. Lower heat and cook covered till onions are soft.
4. Sprinkle with coriander leaves and serve.

ONIONS: Medieval Medicine – Onion poultices were once thought to be a sure way to better vision.

Corn Fritters

1 tin corn

1½ cups flour

½ teaspoon salt

½ teaspoon baking powder

1 egg yolk

A dash of chilli powder

1. Drain the contents of a corn tin, measuring out a breakfast cupful. Chop this up and add 1 ½ teacups of flour sieved with half a level teaspoonful of salt, the same of baking powder and a dash of chilli powder.
2. Add a well beaten egg yolk and lastly fold in the stiffly beaten egg white. Fry delicately brown in spoonfuls in deep hot fat.
3. Serve garnished with fried tomatoes or mushrooms or both.

Banana Mayonnaise

2 bananas

1 lettuce

½ cup mayonnaise

1 tablespoon chopped walnuts

1 orange

1. Slice the bananas lengthwise and arrange them on a bed of lettuce, then coat with the mayonnaise and sprinkle the chopped walnut over them.
2. Peel the orange, divide it into quarters and arrange between bananas.

Sweet and Sour Paneer with Sprouted Dal

½ kg paneer (cut into fingers)

2 cups tomato ketchup

1 onion sliced

8 cloves garlic, chopped

4 green chillies (cut each into 2 long strips)

2 tablespoons cornflour

1 teaspoon red chilli powder

½ cup vinegar

1 teaspoon soya sauce

1 teaspoon Aji-no-moto

1 cup water

1 cup sprouted dal

Postman oil as required

For the batter

½ cup refined flour
1 egg
½ teaspoon Aji-no-moto
Salt and pepper
1 cup water

1. Make a thick batter with the above given batter ingredients.
2. Heat oil in a frying pan, dip the cheese fingers and fry until golden brown. Drain, and keep aside.
3. Mix 2 cups tomato ketchup, 1 cup water, corn flour, red chilli powder, vinegar, soya sauce, garlic, salt and Aji-no-moto to a smooth mixture. Cook this sauce gently on a slow fire until it thickens.
4. Heat oil in a pan, add the chopped garlic, green chillies, fry until light brown. Stir in the prepared sauce and cook for 5 minutes.
5. Add fried paneer fingers, onion and sprouted dal. Cook for another 5 minutes. Serve hot with rice pullao.

French Fried Potatoes

3 medium-sized potatoes

Oil to fry

Salt and pepper to taste

1. Wash and pare potatoes and cut each potato half an inch thick, lengthwise into long fingers.
2. Dry between towels and deep fry in fat.

   Serves 3.

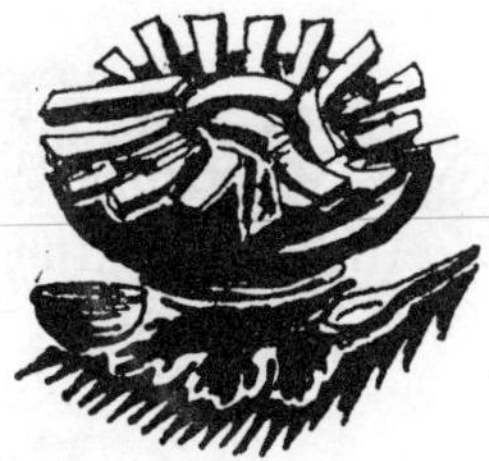

Fried Loki (Burmese)

(Fried White Gourd)

1 loki of about 1.25 kg

1 cup flour

½ cup gram (besan) flour

Water to mix batter

Salt to taste

Oil (about 4 cups)

1. Slice loki crosswise and cut into finger lengths of 1 inch thickness.
2. Make a thick batter of gram powder, flour and turmeric powder, salt and water.
3. Heat the oil taking care that it does not smoke. Dip each piece into the batter and place in the oil one by one. Fry till golden brown.
4. It is good with Burmese coconut rice and chicken curry.

   Serves about 6-8.

Riced Potatoes

½ kg potatoes

¼ teaspoon paprika (or mild chilli powder)

2 teaspoons finely chopped parsley

Boil the potatoes plainly and dry them well. Press them through a heated potato masher into a heated dish. Allow them to fall gently and fork them lightly into place, avoiding crushing them. Sprinkle with paprika and finely chopped parsley.

Serve with creamed chicken. (*See recipe under Fowl, Fish and Meat.*)

Harvard Beets

12 beets, medium size

1 tablespoon sugar

1 teaspoon salt

1 tablespoon flour

½ cup orange juice

1 tablespoon butter

1. Cook beets until tender, peel and cut in ½ inch cubes.
2. Mix sugar, flour, salt and juice thoroughly in saucepan.
3. Add diced beets, and cook slowly until transparent, about 15 minutes.
4. Add butter and serve hot.

Canned beets can be used in place of fresh ones.

Serves 6.

Mushroom Curry (Burmese)

500 gm mushrooms
4 cloves garlic
1 onion, chopped fine
1 large onion, sliced
2 blades of lemon grass (optional)
Salt to taste
1 teaspoon turmeric (haldi) powder
2 tablespoons cooking oil
Juice of ½ a lime

1. Clean and quarter the mushrooms.
2. Pound or mince garlic, chopped onion and lemon grass to a coarse paste.
3. Heat the oil, add turmeric powder, the coarse paste and the sliced onion.
4. Add the mushrooms and simmer over a low fire until they are tender.
5. Squeeze lime-juice over the dish and serve.
   Serves 4.

Creamed Peas

2 cups cooked fresh green peas
1 cup white sauce
Salt and pepper

Mix peas with white sauce. Reheat and serve. It will go well with mutton chops and fried potatoes.

CHEESE MOULDS

¼ cup fresh bread crumbs

1 tablespoon flour

1 egg

1 cup milk

1 teaspoon homemade mustard

Seasonings: salt and pepper

¾ cup grated cheese

Lettuce or watercress garnish

1. Mix the bread crumbs and flour in a saucepan and stir in the beaten egg and milk gradually.
2. Cook over gentle heat, stirring, add seasonings and cheese and stir until boiling.
3. Pour into wetted moulds and allow to set.
4. Unmould carefully and serve on a bed,of lettuce or watercress.

   Serves 4.

Spinach with Cheese

4 cups spinach

2 tablespoons chopped parsley

4 tablespoons fat or butter

½ teaspoon paprika (or mild chilli powder)

4 eggs

2 cups milk

1 cup grated cheese

1 teaspoon salt

1. Wash and chop the spinach.
2. Add the parsley and cook in the fat for ten minutes.
3. Add well-beaten eggs to the milk, and pour over the spinach.
4. Add cheese and seasonings – turn into greased baking dish and bake in a moderate over (350-400°F) for 15 to 20 minutes.
5. Garnish with some cooked shrimps (if liked).

Spicy Cheese Dip

1 cup mayonnaise

1 teaspoon prepared mustard

6 tablespoons cottage cheese

½ teaspoon lemon juice

1. Blend all ingredients together
2. Refrigerate until needed.
3. Use as a dip for any dippery for drinks.
4. You will want to provide cooktail size napkin for each guest.

Dietetic Fruit Dish (Muesli)
Apple Muesli

2 or 3 small applies (or 1 big one)

1 tablespoon walnuts or almonds (ground)

1 level tablespoon Quaker oats (soaked beforehand for 12 hours in 3 tablespoons water)

1 tablespoon condensed milk

Juice of ½ lemon

1. Clean apples by rubbing them with a dry cloth, but do not take away peel, core or pips.
2. Mix condensed milk and lemon juice with oats, quickly grate apples into this and in order to prevent the apples from losing their whiteness through contact with the air immediately.
3. Prepare just before serving. Nuts are served separately and sprinkled over the dish the last moment.

Cooked Radishes with Cheese

1. Boil small pink radishes after the leaves have been removed.
2. Drain, and cook in a saucepan with butter grated cheese until the cheese is melted.

SANDWICHES

They were named after the eighteenth century Earl of Sandwich. The Earl, an ardent gambler, not wishing to rise from the gambling table even for meals, desired the preparation of chunks of meat between the slices of bread to satisfy him and his partners' appetites. Sandwiches, always a standby, can be made the night before to avoid a rush the following day. Well wrapped in foil (or wax paper) stored in a refrigerator or cold larder, they will keep moist and fresh for up to 12 hours.

Cheese and Banana Sandwiches

1 cup cream cheese
1/4 cup cream
2 bananas
1/4 cup mayonnaise
8 buttered bread

Place ice cold bananas, sliced and covered with mayonnaise between buttered slices of white bread spread with cream cheese softened with the cream.
Serves 4.

Golden Ham Sandwiches

8 thick slices (about 2 oz. each) uncooked or cooked ham
Dried bread crumbs
1 cup grated cheese
1 onion, chopped finely
Butter
½ cup grated apple

1. Place four slices of ham on a heat-proof dish and spread over them the apples, cheese and onion.
2. Place rest of the slices on top, spread with a little butter and sprinkle with dried bread crumbs.
3. Bake for 20 minutes.
   Serves 4.

Egg Sandwiches

4 hard boiled eggs
Salt and pepper
Pickles, if desired
A little red chilli powder
8 buttered slices of either white or brown bread

Slice the eggs and place between the buttered slices of bread. Season with salt and pepper and chilli powder and add a layer of pickles if desired. These are good as travel or picnic lunches.
Serves 5.

Sandwiches with Chicken Left-Overs

1. Mix pieces of chicken with a thick white sauce.
2. Mix the chicken with scrambled egg and use as a filling on hot toast and in sandwiches.

Date and Nut Sandwiches

(Use either white or brown bread)

½ cup dates (finely chopped)

½ cup nuts, either cashewnuts or walnuts (finely chopped)

½ cup grated cheese

1 teaspoon lime juice

Mix together the dates, nuts and grated cheese. Moisten with ½ teaspoon lemon juice. Use as sandwich filling.

Coconut-Cashewnut Sandwiches

½ cup fresh grated coconut

½ cup ground cashewnuts

2 tablespoons orange marmalade

Mix together the grated coconut and ground cashewnut. Add 2 tablespoons orange marmalade and blend. Use as sandwich filling.

Peanut Butter and Pickle Sandwiches

½ cup peanut butter

½ cup chopped pickle (mixed pickle is best with peanut)

¼ cup cream

8 slices of bread

Blend together the peanut butter, cream and chopped pickle. Use as filling between the buttered slices of bread.

Serves 4.

Cucumber Sandwiches

Chop and peel cucumber and mix with mayonnaise. Use between thin slices of brown or white bread.

Chicken and Egg Sandwiches

2 egg yolks

1 teaspoon melted butter

1 teaspoon lemon juice

1 cup minced, cooked chicken

Salt and pepper to taste

1 teaspoon dry mustard

10 slices of white or brown bread

1 green chilli (chopped).

Cook the eggs for thirty minutes in water just below boiling point. Take out the yolks and mash as fine as possible. Add melted butter, lemon juice, minced chicken, salt, pepper and mustard. Mix well together. Use the paste to make sandwiches.

Serves 5.

Tuna Sandwiches Deluxe

1 tin of tuna (in chunks)
1 tablespoon grated onion
¼ cup finely chopped parsley or celery
3 hard-boiled eggs
1 teaspoon curry powder
12 slices of bread (white or brown)
1 tablespoon mayonnaise

1. Mix in a bowl the tuna (drained), onion and parsley.
2. Chop the hard-boiled eggs and add to the tuna mixture.
3. Mix well the mayonnaise and curry powder, and blend into the tuna mixture.
4. Use to make sandwiches with brown or white bread.
   Serves 6.

Cream Cheese-Raisin Sandwiches

12 slices of either white or brown bread
¾ cup raisins
¾ cup water
½ cup cream cheese
3 tablespoons milk
1 tablespoon mayonnaise

1. Soak the raisins in ¾ cup water for 30 minutes. Pour off the liquid.
2. Blend the cream cheese with the milk and mayonnaise. Add the soaked and drained raisins.
3. Use to make sandwiches with either white or brown bread.
   Serves 6.

Cheese and Orange Marmalade Sandwiches

½ cup cream cheese

¼ cup cream

½ cup orange marmalade

Salt to taste

8 buttered slices of white or brown bread

Spread cheese over half the slices of buttered bread with the cheese softened with the cream cheese and seasoned with salt if desired, and spread the other slices with orange marmalade. Press the slices together.

Serves 4.

Sardine-Cream Cheese Sandwiches

2 tablespoons butter

1 can of sardines

½ cup cream cheese

1 tablespoon tomato ketchup

½ tablespoon lime juice

12 slices of either white or brown bread

Combine and blend 2 tablespoons butter with the sardines, ½ cup cream cheese, 1 tablespoon tomato ketchup and ½ tablespoon lime juice.

Use to make sandwiches with either white or brown bread.

Serves 6.

Salad Loaf

1 loaf bread (1 lb)

1 cup cooked chicken (chopped)

1 cup cooked ham (chopped)

2 cups mayonnaise

Salt and pepper

Cream cheese

1. Trim crusts from loaf of day old bread, slice off the top and scoop out inside, leaving a ¾ inch shell all around.
2. Fill with chicken and ham mixed with mayonnaise, replace and tie on top slice and chill.
3. Frost with seasoned cream cheese and chill again.
4. Serve on a platter and slice like a loaf of bread.

Curried Chicken-Ham Sandwiches

125 gms butter

2 teaspoons curry powder

½ teaspoon lemon juice

16 slices of brown or white bread

8 slices ham

1 broiler (roasted and sliced)

1. Cream 125 gm butter with 2 teaspoons curry powder and ½ teaspoon lemon juice. Blend until smooth.
2. Spread on 16 slices of bread.
3. Arrange a thin slice each of smoked ham and cooked chicken as filling.

   Serves 8.

Fried Hot Sandwiches

These can be made in either of the following two ways:

1. Make sandwiches of bread and butter and your favourite cheese. Cut into fingers and fry until crisp and brown.
2. Sandwich cheese between slices of bread, soak in beaten egg for a few minutes, then fry.

Almond-Chicken Sandwiches

2 tablespoons butter
$^1/_3$ cup ground salted almonds
1 cup finely chopped cooked chicken
2 tablespoons seedless green grapes (cut up fine)
1 tablespoon mayonnaise
A dash of salt

1. Combine and blend the butter, ground salted almonds, chopped cooked chicken, chopped green grapes, a dash of salt and add mayonnaise to blend.
2. Use to make sandwiches with white or brown bread.

Sardine-Cream Cheese Sandwiches

2 tablespoons butter

1 can sardine

½ cup cream cheese

1 tablespoon tomato ketchup

½ tablespoon lemon juice

12 slices of either white or brown bread

Combine and blend 2 tablespoons butter, 1 can sardine, ½ cup cream cheese, ½ tablespoon tomato ketchup and ½ tablespoon lemon juice.

Serves 6.

Sweet Corn Sandwich

2 slices hot buttered toast

1 egg

Salt and pepper

2 tablespoons tinned corn

½ Oz butter

1 tablespoon milk

Slice of ham or tongue

1. Warm the butter in a small saucepan, drain the corn and add it, also a beaten egg, the milk and a sprinkling of salt and pepper, stir constantly until it thickens.
2. Make the ham hot under a grill or in a frying pan.
3. Put it on a slice of hot buttered toast, spread with the corn mixture and put the remaining piece of toast on the top.

DIPS

Curry Dip (Bahamas)

¼ pint mayonnaise
1 level tablespoon good curry powder
3 tablespoonfuls lemon juice
1 tablespoonful chutney (if liked)
A few drops of tabasco sauce
1 tablespoonful cream
Bread sticks

1. Mix the curry powder, lemon juice, dash of tabasco sauce, chutney, and cream together, then gradually stir in the mayonnaise.
2. Have a glass full of bread sticks beside the dip for guests to help themselves.
3. To make a more exotic dip, instead of bread sticks serve 'fruit sticks'. Cut finger-sized pieces of any firm fruits, such as melon, pineapple, apple, pear and banana, chill them thoroughly, and place them on a plate round the curry dip.

Cheese Balls

4 tablespoons cheese (grated)

4 tablespoons boiled and mashed potatoes

1 egg

12 cashewnuts (fried and chopped)

A pinch of salt, chilli powder

Pepper and bread crumbs

1. Pass the potatoes, cheese and nuts through a mincer so that they are finely grained.
2. Season it with salt, pepper and chilli powder.
3. Form into tiny balls and dip into beaten egg then into the bread crumbs. Roll well and fry to a golden brown colour.

Summer Special

Roll cream cheese balls in chopped mint. They look and taste cool.

1. Cut half-inch slices of white bread into half-inch strips (cut off the crust).
2. Roll in melted butter then grated cheese. Brown lightly in the oven.

Ham and Marmalade Spread

1 cup ground cooked ham

¼ cup mayonnaise

1 tablespoon orange marmalade

½ teaspoon dry mustard

1. Blend 1 cup ground cooked or ready to eat smoked ham, ¼ cup mayonnaise, 1 tablespoon orange marmalade and ½ teaspoon dry mustard.
2. Use either white or brown bread.

Pineapple Dip

1 tin pineapple chunks

Shredded cheddar cheese (or Amul cheese)

Flaked fresh coconut

1. Spear pineapple chunks with picks.
2. To serve – arrange pineapple chunks on tray with bowls of shredded cheese and flaked coconut nearby. Guests do the dipping.

Salami Kababs

16 stuffed olives r

16 salami slices

16 canned pineapple chunks

16 toothpicks

1. On each of the 16 picks, string on olives, and then salami slices folded in quarters, then a pineapple chunk.
2. Refrigerate till serving time.

Watermelon Cocktail

2 cups watermelon balls

Fresh mint

Powdered sugar

2 tablespoons lemon juice

1. With a vegetable cutter prepare small balls of bright pink watermelon.
2. Sprinkle with sugar and add lemon juice.
3. Chill thoroughly. Fill the glasses.
4. Garnish with sprigs of fresh mint.

The watermelon is a member of the cucumber family, and came to be known in India a good 2000 years ago.

Celery and Ham

1. Stuff small stalks of celery with ham (chopped) combined with mayonnaise enough to make it easy to handle.
2. Wrap celery in very thin slices of fresh bread and fasten with toothpick.

Bacon, Peanut Butter Dip

Spread round of thin toast with peanut butter and sprinkle with chopped crisp bacon.

Sardine Strips

1 tin of sardines
Pepper and salt
Cayenne pepper (or little red chilli powder)
4 pieces of buttered toast
Egg yolk
Chopped parsley

1. Pound the sardine and season well.
2. Spread on strips of butter toast and decorate with sieved, hardboiled egg yolk and a little finely chopped parsley.

Dates and Nut Spread

½ cup finely chopped dates

½ cup finely chopped nuts

¼ cup mayonnaise

½ teaspoon lemon juice

1. Mix ½cup finely chopped dates, ½ cup finely chopped nuts and ¼cup mayonnaise.
2. Moisten with ½ teaspoon lemon juice.
3. Use either white or brown bread.

Speedy Tuna Dunk

½ cup soft butter or margarine

½ cup chopped stuffed olives

1 can (1 cup) tuna

1. Cream butter with olives and tuna until well blended.
2. To serve – arrange in bowl, along with any dippers.
3. Let guests drink their own.

Cheddar Dip

2 cups cheddar cheese (if not available use Amul cheese)

½ cup cream

1 teaspoon prepared mustard

3 to 4 apples

1. Add cheese, cream and mustard.
2. Beat with electric mixer or blender until almost smooth.
3. Cut apples in slices and arrange around the bowl of cheese dip.

Overstuffed Eggs

6 hard-boiled eggs

½ cup mayonnaise

1 cup (chopped ham)

Some grated cheese

1. Halve the 6 hard-boiled eggs.
2. Stuff with a mixture of mashed yolks, ½ cup mayonnaise, 1 cup devilled ham and some cheese if you like.

   Serves 6.

Shrimp Butter

¼ cup butter
1 cup ground cooked shrimp
2 teaspoons lime juice
¼ teaspoon grated onion
½ teaspoon minced parsley (optional)
A dash of salt

1. Combine all ingredients.
2. Spread on assorted crackers, toasted bread rounds, large potato chips and melba toast.
3. Garnish with paprika (a dash of mild chilli powder).
4. Or serve in a bowl on a tray or platter with assorted crackers.

Chilli Toast

3 tablespoons butter
2 yolks of egg
¼ cup cream
4 green chillies chopped fine
2 green chillies pounded
1 tablespoon tomato puree or sauce

Mix all together over a low heat until nearly set. Spread on buttered toast and serve hot.

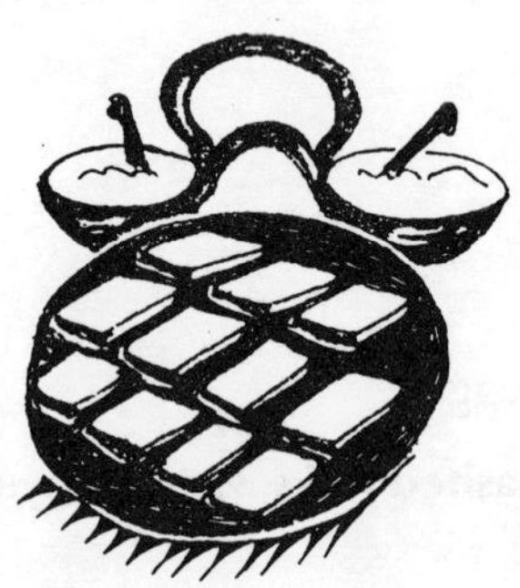

Shrimp on Toast (Chinese)

250 gm fresh shrimp (washed and cleaned)
4 tablespoons onions (chopped finely)
½ teaspoon salt and a dash of pepper to taste
1 egg white (unbeaten)
1 teaspoon cornflour

1. Wash and chop very fine 250 gm fresh shrimps and 4 tablespoons chopped onions; season with ½ teaspoon salt and a dash of pepper.
2. Add 1 unbeaten egg white and 1 teaspoon cornflour. Mix well.
3. Spread on thin squares of bread and fry in deep oil until golden brown. Serve hot.
4. Cut them very small for hors d'oeuvres.
   Serves 4 to 6.

Curry Relish

250 gm fish roe (grilled)
2 tablespoons curry powder
Olive oil or salad oil

Pound the fish roe with a little oil to moisten. Add curry powder and mix thoroughly until smooth.
Spread on buttered fingers of toast.

Cheese Popcorn

Heat packaged popcorn with butter, then toss with grated cheese (with cheddar or Amul cheese)

Mango Fool

Green mangoes
A dash of salt
Sugar to taste

Wash, peel and boil the mangoes in a little water till pulpy. Strain and add salt and sugar to taste, thin with water and chill.

Simple Fruit Cocktail

Mix equal quantities of grapefruit and orange juice. Chill thoroughly, then add a little chopped mint and serve.

Plum Juice

Wash and boil the plums in a little water till pulpy. Strain and add salt and sugar to taste, thin with water and chill.

SWEETS AND PUDDINGS

PEACH MELBA

1 tin peach halves
½ cup raspberry jam
¼ cup peach syrup
2 cups vanilla ice-cream
1 level teaspoon cornflour

1. Blend cornflour with peach syrup and stir into the jam.
2. Cook over moderate heat until mixture is thick and clear, stirring all the time. Allow to cool.
3. Place generous portions of ice-cream in each dish, top with peach halves and coat with melba sauce.

The Story of Peach Melba

Dame Nellie Melba (a famous Austrian singer) was staying at the Savoy Hotel. She returned one night to the hotel with a few friends after giving a concert at the Covent Garden Opera house and expressed a desire for something sweet for supper.

The maitre d' went to the pastry department and prepared the above sweet.

This dish so delighted the Austrian singer that she was curious to know its name – the chef who had invented it, on the spur of the moment, replied 'Peach Melba'.

Floating Island

4 eggs

3 tablespoons sugar

1 kg milk

1 tablespoon custard powder

Some fried almonds for garnish

1 tablespoon sugar for egg-whites

Juice of a lemon quarter

1. Make a thin custard with the egg yolks, 3 table-spoons sugar and the milk. Whip the egg-whites, fold in the rest of the sugar. Pour the custard into an ovenproof dish. Put spoonfuls of the egg-white balls on it. Bake in a hot oven for 5 minutes or steam the egg-white balls in the same milk before putting on the custard.
2. Garnish with chopped fried almonds.

BRANDY RINGS

1 1/3 cups butter

3/4 cup sugar

1½ cups flour

3 tablespoons brandy

Mix all ingredients and work until smooth. Turn onto floured baking board and roll into thin lengths, twisting 2 and 2 together like twine, cut in 4-5 pieces and shape into rings. Place on buttered baking sheet and bake until golden yellow.

BANANA BREAD

½ cup butter

1 cup sugar

2 eggs

1 cup mashed ripe banana

1 teaspoon lemon juice

2 cups sifted flour

3 teaspoons baking powder

½ teaspoon salt

1 cup nuts (chopped)

1. Cream butter and sugar together.
2. Beat eggs until light and add mashed bananas, pressed through a sieve, then add lemon juice. Blend with creamed mixture.
3. Sift flour, baking powder and salt together and mix quickly into the banana mixture. Add nuts, bake in greased loaf pan in moderate oven (375ºF) for about 1½ hours. Makes 1 loaf. Serve with butter.

   Serves 4 to 6.

BANANA FRITTERS

2 large bananas
125 gm flour
2 eggs
A little milk

1. Two large ripe bananas mashed to a pulp and added to a thick batter made with 125 gm flour and 2 eggs, together with a little milk if necessary.
2. Mix well and drop a dessert spoonful of the mixture into deep boiling fat. Cook to a golden brown, drain and serve well-dusted with castor sugar.
   Serves 2 to 4.

PINEAPPLE FROMAGE (Sweden)

2½ cans pineapple
Juice of half a lemon (large size)
½ cup sugar
2 eggs
½ tablespoon gelatine soaked in 3 tablespoons cold water
2 cups heavy whipped cream
A few cherries

1. Beat egg yolks and sugar until fluffy. Add lemon, pineapple juice and gelatine dissolved over hot water to egg mixture and stir until thick. Fold in stiffly beaten egg white, cream and pineapple cubes and pour into mould rinsed in cold water.
2. Keep in refrigerator for 2 hours, before unmoulding and serving. Garnish with pineapple slices and cherries and serve with whipped cream.

Did you know that bananas are called 'Fruits of Paradise' in the Koran? Alexander the Great announced that he had discovered bananas in the Indus Valley in 327 B.C.

CONDENSED MILK TOFFEE

1 tin condensed milk

1 tin fresh milk

100 gm butter

250 gm sugar

5 teaspoons Nescafe coffee powder

1. Cook all ingredients together and boil till it leaves the sides of the pan.
2. Heat and set in buttered plates. Cut into small squares.
3. Add some fried coarsely chopped walnuts if desired.

DATE AND WALNUT FUDGE (Middle East)

500 gm dates

500 gm walnuts

1 cup whipped cream

Stone and chop about 500 gm of dates. Mix with the same quantity of minced and blanched walnuts. Pound until the mixture is smooth, cut into shapes and serve with whipped cream.

Icecream Cakewiches

1 loaf (500 gm) cake

500 gm packet ice cream (vanilla or strawberry)

Slice 1 oz loaf cake in ½ inch slices. Cut the pre-packed ice cream in 8 equal slices. Alternate slices of cake with ice cream on serving plates (2 each)and top with chocolate sauce.

Serves 4.

Treacle Syrup

2 kg gur or jaggery

6 breakfast cups hot water

1 tablespoon lime juice

1. Break up 2 kg of *gur* into a large pan, add 6 large breakfast cups of hot water, boil on a moderate fire, stirring all the while and removing the scum that rises.
2. When it begins to thicken, add 1 teaspoon bicarbonate of soda gradually and stir constantly to prevent the treacle from boiling over the sides of the pan.
3. Strain through a coarse towel and add 1 tablespoon lime juice.

Date Pudding

2 eggs, well beaten
1 cup brown sugar or treacle
1 cup dates, cut in pieces
1 teaspoon baking powder
2 tablespoons flour
1 cup nutmeats (peanuts or cashewnuts)
Whipped cream

1. Mix in the order given. Put the mixture into greased pie-dish.
2. Bake in a moderate slow oven for 30 minutes.
3. Serve with cream.
   Serves 4 to 6.

Fruit Pudding (Sweden)

1 cup sugar
1 cup flour
¼ teaspoon salt
1 teaspoon baking powder
2 cans fruit cocktail (not juice)
½ cup brown sugar (if not available use white sugar)
2 teaspoons chopped nuts (almonds or cashewnuts)
Whipped cream

1. Mix sugar with flour, salt and baking soda. Add mixture to fruit.
2. Cover with brown sugar and nuts.
3. Bake for 1 hour until brown.
4. Top with whipped cream.
5. Serve warm or cold.
   Serves 6 to 8.

Sultana Pudding

1 cup flour
½ cup butter
½ cup sugar
½ cup sultanas
½ teaspoonful baking powder
1 egg
About 1 tablespoon milk (add more if needed)
Whipped cream

1. Decorate a greased bowl with the cleaned sultanas.
2. Cream the butter and sugar well, then add the egg and little flour and beat thoroughly.
3. Add the rest of the flour, the sultanas and the baking powder and mix well. Add a little milk.
4. The pudding mixture should drop easily from a spoon.
5. Turn it into the prepared bowl, cover with greased paper and steam steadily for one and a half hours.
6. Turn the pudding out and serve with whipped cream.
   Serves 4 to 6.

Banana Cream (As served in Belgium)

2 or 3 bananas
½ cup yoghurt
2 tablespoons cream
1 dessertspoonful sugar or mixed fruit jam \
2 egg whites
Cashewnuts (chopped)

1. Mash the bananas and mix well with yoghurt, cream and sugar or mixed jam
2. Whip egg white until stiff, fold into the mixture. Serve in glasses.
3. Garnish with chopped, roasted cashewnuts.

CARAMEL SQUARE (Chinese)

½ cup butter

½ cup sugar

3 egg yolks

1 egg white

1 teaspoon vanilla essence

1 cup sifted flour with 1 teaspoon baking powder

½ teaspoon salt and 3 tablespoons milk

¾ cup cashewnuts or any nuts (finely cut)

1. Cream together ½ cup butter and ½ cup sugar. Add 3 egg yolks and 1 egg white, beat well. Add 1 teaspoon vanilla, 1 cup flour sifted with 1 teaspoon baking powder, ¼ teaspoon salt and 3 tablespoons milk.

2. Spread the mixture in a well greased pan, about 12" x 8" x 2". Sprinkle with ¾ cup nuts, finely cut.

3. Beat 2 egg whites until stiff. Add 1¾ cups sugar and ½ teaspoon vanilla. Spread this mixture over the nuts. Bake about 30 minutes 350°F. Cut into squares while warm.

   Makes 15 squares.

Garlic Bread

1 large French loaf

1-4 cloves of garlic

250 gm butter

1. If only a faint flavour of garlic is desired, cut 4 garlic cloves into halves and mix them into the softened butter. Leave for several hours, then remove the garlic before spreading the butter on the bread.
2. If a stronger flavour is liked, chop all cloves very finely, squash them with a little salt with the blade of knife and mix into the butter thoroughly. Leave for a few hours.
3. Cut the loaf into ½ inch slices on the slant, but not right through the bottom. Open each slice and spread on one side with the garlic butter, then press the whole loaf together again and wrap in foil and place it in the oven for 15-20 minutes.

   Serves 8.

Coffee Jelly

4 cups milk

2 tablespoons water

2 tablespoons Nescafe coffee

3 teaspoons gelatine

250 gm sugar

1 teaspoon vanilla essence

1. Heat milk and stir in coffee.
2. Soak gelatine in water for 5 minutes and add with sugar to milk. Cook for ¼ hour, stirring well.
3. Add vanilla essence and pour into individual dishes or glass bowls.
4. Decorate with chopped almonds and whipped cream when set.

Coconut Custard (Malayan)

2 cups coconut milk (from 1 large coconut)
500 gm sugar
4 eggs
Essence of rose
Whipped cream

1. Scrape the coconut and place in a bowl. Pour over it half a cup of cold water and leave for ten minutes. Transfer the coconut flakes into a muslin bag or a colander and press the milk from the flakes. It should make two cups. If not sufficient a little more water can be added to the flakes and they are pressed again.
2. Beat the eggs and sugar till light and creamy. Add the coconut milk and mix well together. Pour into a greased mould, cover with greased paper and steam about an hour. Serve chilled with whipped cream.

   Serves 4-6.

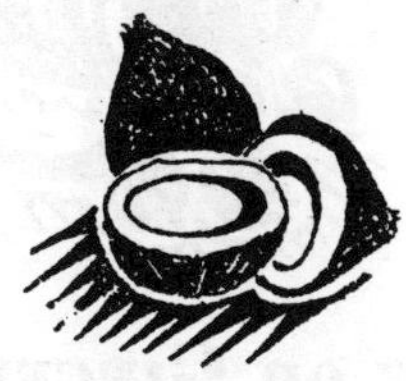

Mocha Coffee (Austria)

2 cups strong coffee
3 cups milk
125 gm cooking chocolate
½ cup sugar
Whipped cream

1. Strain the coffee, mix it with 2 cups of hot milk.
2. Dissolve the chocolate and the sugar in 1 cup milk. Stir the chocolate mixture into the coffee.
3. This can be beaten until froothy and served hot with whipped cream.

Pumpkin and Walnuts (Middle East)

This is a Kurdish dish much eaten in Baghdad.

¾ cup sugar
4 tablespoons water
500 gm pumpkin
½ cup chopped walnuts
Thick cream

1. Cook sugar and the water to a thick syrup.
2. Wash the pumpkin, peel it, remove the seeds and chop the flesh into small pieces.
3. Cook it in the syrup until it is thick and soft and has absorbed almost all the syrup.
4. Arrange the pumpkin in a plate and sprinkle it with the chopped walnuts.
5. Serve with thick cream.

   Serves 6.

Brandy or Ginger Snaps

2 tablespoons plain flour
2 tablespoons butter
2 tablespoons golden syrup
1 tablespoon ground ginger
Whipped cream

Mix syrup and butter in a pan, cool slightly, then stir in flour and ginger. Mix well and place teaspoons of the mixture well apart on greased baking sheets. Bake in a moderate oven for 10-15 minutes. Remove with a palette knife when they are just beginning to get crisp, and roll up – an easy way to do this is around the greased handle of a wooden spoon.

When cold fill with whipped cream.

Burmese Hinjo Soup, Burmese Balachaung, Burmese Pickle-Thanat, Burmese Coconut Blanc-Mange.

Iced Yogurt Soup/Cream of Onion Soup.

Egg and Spinach Mould Salad.

Grape and Pineapple Salad.

Stuffed Tomato Salad.

Burmese Chicken Curry.

Peanut Cookies

1 cup butter
2 cups sugar
1 egg
5 heaped tablespoons plain flour
1 level teaspoon baking powder
½ teaspoon salt
1 tablespoon cocoa
2 cups shelled, skinned peanuts

Cream the butter and sugar, then beat in the egg. Sift the flour, baking powder, salt and cocoa and stir into the creamed mixture. Chop the skinned peanuts and add to the mixture. Put teaspoons of the mixture into greased baking tray and bake in a moderately hot oven for about 15 minutes. Cool on a wire tray.

Burmese Coconut Blanc-Mange

4½ tablespoons cornflour (cornstarch)
1 pint coconut milk
4 tablespoons sugar
A pinch of salt

1. Grate one small coconut and add one pint boiling water, squeeze out the coconut milk in a piece of cloth.
2. Blend cornflour with a little of the coconut milk into a smooth paste. Put remaining coconut milk, sugar and salt in a saucepan and bring to the boil. Pour this into the cornflour paste mixing well.
3. Return to saucepan, stirring constantly as it boils a few minutes. Pour into wet mould. When cool it will become firm.

Brown Bread

1 large cup ata or whole wheat flour
1 tablespoon sugar
1 teaspoon salt
1 egg
1 tablespoon butter
1 teaspoon baking powder
1 cup milk

1. Sift together *ata*, salt and baking powder, then rub in the butter.
2. Beat together sugar and egg. Add milk, then add to the dry ingredients and mix well.
3. Put into a buttered tin and bake in a hot oven or steam.
4. Serve with butter and jam or whipped cream with coconut (freshly grated).
5. This quantity makes a loaf in a Quaker oats tin.
   Serves 6 to 8.

Pineapple Balls

4 tablespoons flour, sifted
2 eggs, well beaten
½ cup pineapple, finely chopped
Milk for mixing the batter
Pinch of salt
Ghee or butter for frying

1. Re-sift the flour with the salt, then add the beaten eggs and just enough milk to make a thick batter.
2. Then mix in the chopped pineapple.
3. Heat the ghee and drop the batter by spoonfuls into it.
4. When the balls become golden brown, drain them and serve immediately with sugar sifted over them.
   Serves 6.

Peach Baskets

1 loaf unsliced bread (white)

1 can condensed milk

1½ cups shredded coconut

6 peach halves

1. Cut 6 slices (¾ inch thick) from bread. Cut off crusts to make 3 inch squares.
2. Scoop shallow 2 inch circle in top of each.
3. Spread top and sides with condensed milk and dip in coconut.
4. Bake on well-greased cooking sheet about 10 minutes till brown.
5. Take from pan and cool on rack.
6. At serving time add peaches on top.
7. Serve with whipped cream.

Serves 6.

Pineapple, tinned or fresh, contains all the properties which enable you to resist colds.

Sago Sweet (Burmese)

1 cup sago

1 cup sugar

1 small coconut grated

3 cups water

Colouring, green or cochineal

1. Bring to a boil the 3 cups of water. Dissolve the sugar and strain to remove sediment. Bring to a boil again.
2. Add sago and boil till it becomes transparent.
3. To make it pale green or pink add colouring to the sago.
4. Pour into shallow pan to cool.
5. When cold, with dessert spoon scoop out portions which are rolled in the grated coconut very slightly and serve.

SAUCES, DRESSINGS AND MISCELLANEOUS

Mayonnaise Salad Dressing

1 egg yolk
1 cup salad oil
1 dessertspoon vinegar
Salt and pepper

Put a carefully broken yolk (no white at all) into a basin. Add the oil, drop by drop, stirring gently all the time. When the sauce begins to thicken stir in the vinegar, salt and pepper. Add more oil drop by drop till it once again thickens, when the oil can be poured in slowly, stirring always, until finished. Taste and add more salt and pepper if you wish. Should the mayonnaise refuse to thicken and look curdled when finished, do not panic. Break a new yolk into another basin and stir the mixture into it slowly.

Homemade Mustard

3 tablespoons dry mustard

1 tablespoon sugar

1 tablespoon flour

½ cup hot vinegar

A few drops of salad oil

A little salt

1. Mix 3 tablespoons dry mustard, 1 tablespoon sugar and 1 tablespoon flour.

2. Add ½ cup hot vinegar and cook until thick stirring constantly to keep homemade mustard fresh, add a few drops of salad oil when mixing to keep from caking, mix in a little salt.

French Dressing

3 tablespoons salad oil or

1 tablespoon vinegar (white)

½ teaspoon salt

½ teaspoon pepper

Mix all together. You can, if you like, add a pinch of sugar and ¼ teaspoon of mustard.

PICKLED PINEAPPLE (To serve with poultry)

1 can pineapple chunks

1 cupful vinegar

½ cupful sugar

1 teaspoonful pickling spices

1. **Drain the syrup from the can, put it in a saucepan with the vinegar, sugar and spices.**
2. **Simmer, strain, then add pineapple chunks.**

TARTAR SAUCE – I

1 cup mayonnaise

1 dessertspoon mustard

1 dessertspoon chopped gherkins and 1 onion (chopped)

A little vinegar

1 dessertspoon chopped capers (optional)

½ teaspoon anchovy sauce

1 diced hardboiled egg

1. Mix the mustard to a very thin paste with vinegar. Add it to the mayonnaise.
2. Mix well with the other ingredients and serve.

   Enough for 4 persons.

Tartar Sauce – II

1 cup mayonnaise

1 onion (chopped finely)

½ teaspoon mint (chopped finely)

2 hard-boiled egg (chopped finely)

Mix 1 cup mayonnaise with chopped onion, chopped mint and chopped boiled egg and serve.

Enough for 4 persons.

Allspice

¼ teaspoon nutmeg

¼ teaspoon cinnamon

1/8 teaspoon cloves

Mix all above ingredients together

Chocolate Sauce

1½ teaspoonfuls of cornflour

1 dessertspoonful of cocoa

1 cup of milk

Sugar and vanilla essence

Mix the corn flour and cocoa to a smooth paste with a small quantity of milk. Heat the remainder and stir into it.

Return to the pan and bring to the boil, add sugar to taste and boil gently for a few minutes to cook the sauce, keeping it well stirred.

Add vanilla and serve.

Butter Sauce

¼ cup fresh Amul butter

1 tablespoon white vinegar

1 small onion

Salt and pepper

1. Peel the onion and mince it very fine. Put it in a small saucepan with the vinegar and cook very gently until about three-quarters has evaporated.
2. Add butter in very small pieces.
3. Serve when very hot with grilled fish or meat or with asparagus.

Celery Sauce

1 head of celery
1 cup milk
1 tablespoon flour
1 tablespoon butter
Small piece of mace (javitri)

1. Take the white part of a head of celery, cut it in small pieces, put it in a saucepan with enough milk to cover it, add the mace. Simmer gently until the celery is quite soft.
2. Then take out the mace, strain off the milk.
3. Blend the flour, butter and milk, add the celery and serve.
   Good with boiled turkey or chicken.

White Sauce

1/4 cup butter
2 tablespoons flour
2 cups hot milk
1 dessertspoon butter

Melt the butter in a saucepan, stir in the flour with a wooden spoon on a low heat, pour over the hot milk gradually, stirring all the time till smooth and creamy, cook gently for a further 2 or 3 minutes. Stir in the 1 dessertspoon butter before serving.

Mushroom Sauce

1 cup white sauce

125 gm mushrooms

200 gm butter

1. Cook the thinly sliced mushrooms very gently in the butter for 15-20 minutes.
2. Stir the mushrooms with the butter and their juice into the hot sauce.
3. Serve with fish and meat entrees, and poultry.

Christmas Pudding Sauce

2 eggs

Quarter cup rum or brandy

Quarter cup water

150 gm castor sugar

1. Whisk all the ingredients in a basin placed over a pan of boiling water.
2. Whisk vigorously all the time until the sauce is thick and frothy.
   Serve at once.

Apple Sauce

½ kg apples
2 tablespoons water
50 gm butter
Rind and juice of ½ lemon
Sugar to taste

1. Stew the apples very gently with the water, butter and lemon rind until they are pulpy. Beat them quite smooth or rub them through a nylon sieve.
2. Reheat the sauce with the lemon juice and sweeten to taste.
3. Serve with roast pork, roast goose or pork sausages.
   Excellent also as a sweet sauce with ginger pudding.

White Wine Sauce

1 cup white stock or fish stock
200 gm butter
100 gm flour
Quarter cup white wine
2 egg yolks
Juice of ½ lemon
Salt and pepper

1. Make a white sauce with the stock, half the butter and the flour.
2. To this add the wine and simmer it for 10 minutes.
3. Whip in the remaining butter just below boiling point, then stir in the egg yolks mixed with lemon juice, season. Thicken the egg yolks without boiling.
4. Serve with fish or white meat.

Mint Sauce

3 heaped tablespoons finely chopped mint

A pinch of salt

2 teaspoons sugar

2 tablespoons boiling water

½ cup vinegar

1. The mint should be young and freshly gathered if possible. Wash well, pick the leaves from the stalks and chop the leaves finely.
2. Mix the mint, salt and sugar in the sauce-boat.
3. Pour onto them the boiling water and leave the mixture to cool.
4. Add the vinegar and if possible leave the sauce for 1 hour to infuse the flavour of mint into the vinegar.
5. Serve with roast lamb.

GINGER SAUCE (Siamese)

10 dried mushrooms

4 tablespoons vinegar (malt)

2 tablespoons chopped spring onions

1 tablespoon cornflour

4 tablespoons sugar

½ cup water

1 tablespoon Chinese soya sauce

4 tablespoons chopped red young ginger

1. Soak mushrooms in water for a few minutes, drain. Chop them fine.
2. Put all the ingredients in a saucepan, except the cornflour, and cook.
3. Blend cornflour with a little water. Pour into the boiling sauce. Stir till cooked.

GINGER PICKLE (Thai)

1. Slice ginger root in thin diagonal slices. Boil enough vinegar to cover in the jar.
2. Add salt and sugar to taste.
3. Pour vinegar when cool over ginger.

   In 3 days it will be ready to use.

   All ingredients depend on the cook as to how much ginger she would like to cook for this pickle.

Cheese Sauce

Add three or four tablespoons of finely grated cheese to 1 cup of white sauce, and stir until melted.

Dream Puris

1 cup flour
25 gm butter
1 tablespoon milk
1/4 teaspoon salt
Postman oil for frying
1 dessertspoon baking powder
1/4 teaspoon sugar

1. Mix flour, salt, sugar and add milk. Mix well together to prepare dough.
2. Divide into balls and roll out into small rounds each of 3 inch diameter.
3. Heat oil and deep fry rounds, gently pressing down with flat spoon in circular motion. When bloated turn rounds over. When light brown, remove rounds from pan.
4. Drain on paper and serve hot.
5. This mixture makes 4 purees.

Mrs Usha Narayanan, the wife of the Vice-President of India, says that the proper way to serve these puris is to put either meat or chicken curry (should be cut into small pieces) in the centre of each puree and on top of the curry put some curd, salad of sliced onion, green chillies, a little paprika and salt. She herself made this dish at Miss Lutters' residence. It is very delicious. Do try it out yourself for the family lunch.

A NOTE ON WINE

Certain kinds of wines go well with certain foods.

1. Soup — Sherry or white wine
2. Fish — White wine or Champagne
3. Fowl — White wine or dry Champagne
4. Turkey — Red Wine
5. Red meat — Red wine (should be slightly warmed)
6. Cheese — Red wine or Port
7. Dessert — Sweet Sherry, Port or Champagne
8. Fruits & Nuts — Port or Tukay
9. Coffee — Creme-de-Mentho, Cognac and other cordials.
10. Champagne is served off the ice, for "great occasions". Champagne is still the accepted wine.
    Learn to choose and serve your fine wines correctly so that they blend with each course to make a perfect meal.

History of Herbs and Spicelore

by Yasmine Betar

The author of "Middle East Recipes".

I am indeed extremely grateful to Mrs Yasmine Betar for her excellent book, which she had very kindly autographed and presented to Padma Shree Miss Lilian Lutter, MBE, OBE in 1968. This book now is a great help to my Simple Cook Book. "Thank you", Mrs Yasmine Betar.

History – Herbs and Spicelore

The following are some of the spices with or little history and folklore of each and their uses. There are over 200 different kinds of spices.
Spices have also been used as a medium of exchange. During the middle ages a sheep was worth a pound of ginger, and two pounds of Mace (Jaitri) would buy a cow.
The best cooks know that the right spices and used skillfully in the right places stimulate appetites, bring out the full flavour of food and digestion. It has been said food with seasoning is talk with reasoning.
It brings back memory of the old nursery rhyme: "What are the little girls made of?" "Sugar and spice and all things nice".

1. **Mustard**
   Used medicinally by the Arab doctors for respiratory illnesses and poultices.

2. **Celery**
   In medieval times celery was cultivated by herbalists for its medical properties, it is rich in mineral salts and important Vitamin C.

3. **Thyme**
   Thyme for Romance – In the middle ages, thyme was a symbol of courage. Fair ladies pinned springs of thyme on their knights. Carried into battle, thyme supposedly waded off stings, arrows and whatever other outrageous fortune came to hand.

4. **Mint**
   Matriculated Mint – Scholars in Biblical time wore wreaths of mint around their heads – They thought it stimulated thinking. Superstitious saying – Have portions of the ancients were considered more effective when mint was a major ingredient.

5. **Bay Leaves (Tez Pati)**
   Aromatic leaves of sweet bay laurel tree. The ancients used to boil the leaves and put it in their bath water. In some areas even today it is boiled with clothing for antiseptic purposes during epidemic. Romans used wreaths of laurel to crown royal head.

6. **Basil (Kali Tulsi)**
   Basil comes from the Greek meaning King, or King Herb. Hindus plant it around their homes and temples to ensure happiness. It was used by ancients to sweeten breath before receiving guests.

7. **Ginger**
Ginger tea to ease an ailing stomach and is still used for that purpose in many parts of the western world.

8. **Garlic**
In ancient days garlic was supposed to be a safe way to avert the evil eye.

9. **Turmeric (Haldi)**
Often used as colouring agent in place of saffron. Ancient spice used as perfume as well as spice.

10. **Clove (Loong)**
Chinese writings from the third century B.C. state that officers of the court were compelled to hold cloves in their mouths when addressing the sovereign. Clove oil stimulates flow of gastric juices and is not injurious to the lining of the stomach.

11. **Cinnamom (Dal Cheene)**
Has a medical reputation as a sure for colds and its strong antiseptic action is particularly evident in the spice where the workers are said to be singularly free from chest troubles owing to the inhalation of the fragrant breezes. Some people brew tea with cinnamom sticks. Popular in Lebanon – also served as a drink in celebration of a child's first tooth in some villages.

12. **Cardamom (Elachi)**
There are many stories told of the old "Coffee" shop folklore origin. Poets of the ancient East world weave their stories long into the night, stimulated by the hot coffee and cardamom.

13. **Poppy Seeds (Khus Kus)**
Statistical statement – It takes about 900,000 poppy seeds to make a pound – wonder who counted them – And why?

14. **Saffron (Kesar)**
Did you know that it takes somewhere around 70,000 flowers to yield a pound of saffron? King Solomn grew them.

15. **Mace (Jaitri) Nutmeg (Jaiphal)**
In the 15th century Nutmeg was used as a fumigant in the streets of Rome. Its tea was supposed to cure insomnia.

16. Fenugreek Seed (Methi)
The ancients prized this seed because of its stimulating action on the digestion. An old Egyptian remedy called for the seed to be soaked in water until swelled into a thick paste and used in soothing fevers.

17. Lentils
There is an old tale of folklore origin that the students and wise men of old ate lentils containing a good deal of protein, iron and other minerals and one as source of quick energy and growth.

18. Cumin Seed (Zeera)
Small dried fruit of the parsley. Flavouring is used with cabbage dishes. According to some health enthusiastic it makes cabbage more digestible.

19. Curd or Yoghurt
Curd is considered a great health food and is also used for controlled diet today. A good hot weather dish. Also, recommended by some doctors for in between snacks, especially good in salads – healthful and satisfying.